Every House a Frontier

"Every house in the territory of Michigan is a frontier, there are no back settlements nor will the country admit of any."

DUNCAN MCARTHUR

Commandant at Detroit, to James Monroe, Secretary of War, Feb. 6, 1815

Courtesy of the Burton Historical Collection, Detroit Public Library

DETROIT IN 1818

Every House
A Frontier

Detroit's Economic Progress

1815–1825

FLOYD RUSSELL DAIN

DETROIT   WAYNE UNIVERSITY PRESS   1956

This publication is made possible by

THE DETROIT EDISON FUND

*established in the
History Department of Wayne University
for the publication of works in local history*

Preface

Late in 1815, 114 years after its founding, the chief wilderness bastion of the Old Northwest was incorporated as the City of Detroit. One would expect that this action represented a significant advancement in the growth and prosperity of the old town, but such was not the case. Detroit had been a prime objective in the campaigns of the War of 1812, which had ended recently, and had been subjected to the ravages associated with conquest and reconquest. The act of incorporation was chiefly an attempt to boost the morale of the townspeople and to promote American settlement. Actually, the new city faced a dismal future. The war had scattered its population, disrupted its economy, reduced it in wealth and real property, and publicized its weaknesses and vulnerability. At the time of its incorporation it was an American city only in the political sense, for most of its inhabitants were Canadian French, and its institutions were for the most part typical of the Old Regime. Geographically, it was separated from the American community by an unbroken wilderness difficult to penetrate, and by a body of water as yet untouched by improvement, unpredictable in its moods, and as hazardous to navigation as the Atlantic coastal waters. Without a developed hinterland to support it, with disgruntled savages encamped in its environs, and with its citizenry threatened by starvation, Detroit entered upon its new career isolated, dependent, and insecure. Ten years and two days after the act of incorporation the resurgent City of Detroit, along with the whole nation, celebrated the completion of the Erie Canal, the engineering miracle which was to have such an enormous impact upon the settlement and development of the Great Lakes region.

v

The interval between these two events comprises a logical and natural unit in a study of the economic history of Detroit. The hopelessness and apathy of the nascent city in October, 1815, was in marked contrast to the anticipation and bustle which characterized Detroit in October, 1825. It is the purpose of this book to point out the complexity of the economic problems confronting the city during these years, and to record the courage, resourcefulness, and enterprise of the citizens and their leaders who succeeded in establishing a new and more stable economy for Detroit during its first decade as a city.

The book was originally submitted to the Graduate Council of Wayne University in April, 1943, as a Master's Thesis. It was written under the capable guidance of Dr. Joe L. Norris of the Department of History and former editor-in-chief of the Wayne University Press, to whom I am indebted for scholarly advice and helpful suggestions. The staff of the Burton Historical Collection, Detroit Public Library, was especially generous of its time and facilities. I am also grateful to the Manuscript and History Division of the New York State Library, Albany, New York, for assistance rendered me in locating source material pertaining to the Erie Canal. Mr. Frederic Douglas of Denver, Colorado, kindly granted me permission to use and to quote from the John R. Williams Letterbook, on deposit in the Burton Collection.

Mr. Alexander Brede, editor of the Wayne University Press, spent considerable time on the manuscript preparing it for publication. I am most appreciative of his penchant for clarity and his meticulous editing. While the manuscript was in preparation, my wife, Carolyn S. Dain, was a constant source of inspiration and encouragement. She has also helped immensely in the difficult task of preparing it for the publisher.

Except for minor revisions in the interest of clarity and some modernization of capitalization, punctuation, and spelling, the text is essentially the same as the thesis submitted to the Wayne University History Department in 1943.

F. R. D.

Table of Contents

Detroit in 1815

The northwestern territories of the United States, the Detroit area in particular, had suffered extremely during the War of 1812. Early in the war, August 16, 1812, a British force under General Brock captured the post, and British troops occupied it for more than a year until Commodore Perry's victory on Lake Erie and the subsequent counter-invasion by the American army under General William Harrison forced the conquerors to evacuate the town and retreat to Canada.[1] The return of the American troops, September 29, 1813, however, did not bring the security that might have been expected. The majority of Harrison's troops were dispatched elsewhere, and a small force was left to rebuild and strengthen the fortifications of the post and to defend it from possible attacks by the British and their Indian allies. Skirmishes with the Indians in the neighborhood and the rumors of British advances on the town kept the garrison on edge and precluded any return to normalcy in the conduct of civilian pursuits.[2]

Insecure and dependent though Detroit had been prior to the war, the return of peace in 1815 found a state of affairs even more hopeless and discouraging.[3] During the period of enemy occupation the city was the victim of weak military administration. The British made little or no effort to control the activities of their Indian allies.[4] Cass claimed that "through fear or policy, the British suffered them to pillage the poor miserable inhabitants at pleasure."[5] The Indians shot down the cattle of the citizens, robbed them of their provisions and clothing, burned fences, barns, and even houses and furniture. All this was done despite a solemn pledge by the British that private property would be held inviolate.[6] Citizens were "crowded from their dwellings by a proud and domineering foe, and jostled in the streets by drunken and bloodthirsty savages." They were intimidated, assaulted, and even murdered.[7]

In addition to these outrages, the inhabitants suffered extreme hardship under the British command. Many citizens of means were exiled and their property confiscated.[8] Others were pressed into British service.[9] Civil law was powerless and soon gave way to martial law.[10] Public morals reached a low ebb.[11] Before evacuating the town the British burned the fort, the barracks, and all public buildings; all public property that could be moved was carried away.[12] So extensive was the destruction and so widespread its effect that in November, 1813, shortly after the Americans re-occupied the town, Cass wrote that "this country is totally exhausted of all its resources, and except as a frontier is scarcely worth possessing."[13]

Nor did the destruction end with the return of the Americans. Until new barracks could be erected, it was necessary to quarter soldiers in the farm homes from which the inhabitants had fled. Since it was inconvenient to transport firewood from the woods a mile or more in the rear of the town, the soldiers added to the despoliation of private property by using flooring, fences, and outbuildings for fuel. Other buildings were torn down to provide the lumber necessary for coffins for the large number of soldiers who perished from disease.[14]

Thus in 1815 the Detroit area was almost completely devastated. The population was in desperate straits for want of food, clothing, and shelter. The little frontier town that had existed for a

hundred and fourteen years as a military post and trading center
was breathing its last. There had to be a new beginning and a
new economy.

A survey of the circumstances confronting the city at this time
indicates that its prospects were far from encouraging. The population, exclusive of the garrison, probably totaled less than a
thousand, and four-fifths of this number were Canadian French.[15]
Early in 1815 Woodbridge wrote: " The people in this country
are in a lamentable condition—if prevented from working their
farms by Indian incursions another season the general distress
will be inconceivable." [16] A month later he informed the Secretary of War that a " considerable proportion " of the inhabitants
had " nothing to plant, nothing to eat, and no money to buy
with." [17] In a letter to Cass, who was visiting in Ohio at the
time, he said:

> The poor French people especially at the Riviere aux Raisin
> are in a condition from all I can learn of real and deplorable
> distress. Had it been possible to have convened a Territorial
> Legislature, I had determined to have submitted to them with
> much interest, however discouraged our fiscal concerns may
> be, a proposition to appropriate a territorial fund for their
> immediate relief, in the hope of an ultimate reimbursement
> by the gen. govt. That object however—is out of the
> question.
> They will get along, how well I do not know, until planting
> time—but it does seem to me indispensible that they should
> be supplied with corn or wheat to plant.[18]

Judge Woodward supported Woodbridge in pleading for federal
relief,[19] and although Cass expressed doubt that their petitions
would receive favorable consideration,[20] he was authorized by the
War Department late in May to expend the sum of $1,500 for
the relief of the sufferers at the River Raisin.[21] Upon investigation,
however, Cass determined that the distress was equally serious
throughout the region and concluded that the money should be

used to help all who were in need. Thereupon, he purchased
flour to the amount of the grant, entrusting its fair distribution
to Father Gabriel Richard.[22] While this measure alleviated the
distress for the moment, more help was necessary. In July Cass
wrote to the War Department recommending that the poor in
the territory be permitted to draw provisions from the government stores. " The country is generally poor," he explained, " and
war while the British were here appeared in its worst forms. It
drained the country of its resources and made it a theater of
individual indigence and distress." He also asked that a " moderate sum " be appropriated " to enable the small families to
purchase wheat for the next seed time." [23]

The War Department acceded to these recommendations,[24]
and late in September Cass sent notices to the several justices of
the peace and the officers of the militia detailing the procedure
whereby they were to determine those eligible to obtain relief.[25]
Relief was particularly welcome to those citizens whose means
of livelihood had been destroyed; and a month later Judge James
Witherell noted that most of the old inhabitants were back in
the city, " but many of them so poor as to draw provisions from
the public stores." [26]

To those interested in promoting the welfare and prosperity
of Detroit, the French element in the population constituted a
source of despair and disillusionment. Prior to the American
occupation of the territory many of the French *habitants* were
engaged in the Indian trade, the returns from which furnished
their chief means of subsistence. Of necessity this trade was
opposed to the development of a more stable agricultural economy
because the trader desired the preservation of the forest to protect
the source of his income.[27] By the very nature of his occupation
he spent half the year working far from home, constantly
threatened by privation and exposure, while he wasted the
remainder of his time in idleness and amusement.[28]

When the British moved their headquarters across the river to

Malden, they offered land grants of two hundred acres to the
French in Michigan who wished to live under British sovereignty.
Many accepted the offer and moved their families to the new
British towns of Sandwich and Amherstburg.[29] According to the
terms of the Jay Treaty concluded in 1794, British concerns were
entitled to trade freely in American territory.[30] Consequently, they
competed strongly with the Americans for the favor of the Indians
and having wider experience and a greater amount of capital
gradually secured a large amount of the trade. The turmoil in
Europe during the Napoleonic period reduced the market for furs,
and the agitated state of relations between the Indians of the
Northwest Territory and the Americans tended to limit their
collections. Thus the importance of Detroit as a trading center
diminished, and with the disappearance of wild life in the area
the profits gleaned from the trade lessened. With its decline
the *habitants* found it increasingly difficult to procure employment,
and, as their sole recourse, turned more to agriculture in an
attempt to eke out a livelihood.[31]

They occupied the shore lands above and below Detroit and
along the nearby streams tributary to the Detroit River. The
typical French farm was a mile and a quarter deep but had narrow
river frontage. The homes along the riverfront were close together, and the expanse from the River Rouge to Lake St. Clair
appeared to one visitor like "the suburbs of a great town."[32]
There was no inland settlement, nor was it believed that the back
country would admit of any.[33]

Agriculture was in a primitive state. In the past the energies
of the population had been chiefly directed toward the fur trade;
benevolent governments, interested in preserving this source of
wealth and in maintaining the post in its strategic location, had
provisioned the garrison and sent aid to the needy. Except for the
garrison, there had been little market for farm produce. Consequently, there was no talented and industrious agricultural group,
and famine or the threat of famine often confronted the area.[34]

The character of the *habitants* intensified the agricultural problem. Those who had engaged in the fur trade had associated with the Indians to such an extent that they had contracted their manners; as a result they neglected their fields, some being so shiftless that they depended upon outside sources for the very bread they ate, even though they possessed acres of cleared land. They were, as a rule, lacking in ambition and satisfied with little. One writer claimed that their "aspirations seldom extended beyond the possession of a canoe, a spear, and a few hooks for fishing, with a rifle, and a half dozen dogs." [35] They were reluctant to accept the advice and to follow the examples of those possessed of greater knowledge, preferring to use the methods pursued by their forebears in cultivating the land. According to Woodbridge they knew nothing of farming and perhaps less of gardening. Instead of fertilizing soils that had been worked for a hundred years or more, they hauled manure on to the ice in the winter so that it would be washed away in the spring. Their equipment was ancient and obsolete. Although their orchards were fruitful and provided them with products for trade and export, they neglected them to such an extent that their continued productivity was threatened. With these shortcomings the French in 1815 made piteous attempts to eke out an existence on their war-ravaged lands. The fact that few of them had legitimate titles to their farms at this time probably tempered the desire to improve them. Investigations to determine the legality of their claims had been going on for many years, but little progress had been made. It was apparent, however, that until more industrious farmers were induced to settle in the territory, or until the French acquired better methods of husbandry, the Detroit area could not be self-providing.[36]

The presence of hundreds of destitute Indians also was a perplexing problem. During the war the Administration had authorized the employment of loyal Indians for military purposes and had guaranteed supplies and provisions for their needs.[37] On

October 18, 1813, shortly after the American reoccupation, an armistice was concluded with the hostile Indians.[38] Nevertheless, for a time it was dangerous to work in the fields near the town or to travel the waterways because of their marauds.[39] Gradually, however, the danger lessened, and even before the conclusion of peace, many of the warriors who had been hostile to the United States straggled into the town with their families, begging for assistance.[40] Deserted by their British allies to whom they had looked for sustenance, they faced privation and death unless the Americans came to their aid.[41] For a time it was difficult to distribute food in sufficient quantity to satisfy their hunger, and large numbers of them roamed the streets, constantly searching for scraps of food. Many others collected in the town to sell their furs, and they could be heard " whooping and shouting in the streets the whole night." [42] With so many former enemies in the neighborhood, the citizens felt insecure, and the repeated disturbances resulting from their presence was a constant concern. Although Colonel Butler and William Woodbridge declared that there was no danger of Indian hostility, the latter suggested that several of the foremost chiefs be sent to Washington to consider peace terms, for their presence in the interior would insure peace on the frontier.[43]

Even after the news arrived in Detroit that the war had ended, the inhabitants were uneasy, for the large numbers of Indians still in the vicinity showed no signs of departing. Many of them were desirious of setting out for their homes, but until they could obtain the clothing and provisions necessary for the journey, they remained encamped about the town, dependent upon government stores for subsistence.[44] Perhaps Witherell best expressed the feelings of the populace in regard to the danger from Indians in a letter to his wife: " Should peace continue, it will be many years before people will feel their scalps quite as safe as in Vermont." [45]

The isolated position of Detroit accentuated the problem of

feeding and supplying its inhabitants. Most of the staple foods were imported from western New York, western Pennsylvania, and Ohio.[46] The disruption of agriculture and commerce by the war, the demands of the garrison, and the necessity of feeding large numbers of Indians caused a shortage of provisions in Detroit. General McArthur left Detroit in November, 1814, in an endeavor to obtain supplies for the troops. Writing from Ohio to the Secretary of War he said: "When I left Detroit, the garrison at that post and Malden subsisted entirely on the resources of the country. Those posts and Fort Gratiot must shortly be abandoned unless supplied from the interior." [47] Butler appealed to Woodbridge to relax the customs regulations preventing two vessels from sailing in order that they might leave immediately to bring food for the garrison and the starving population.[48] During the winter of 1815-1816 the army contractor imported thousands of pounds of flour from Canada, even though a duty of 25 per cent was levied upon it.[49] So inadequate were the transportation facilities between Detroit and other parts of the country that there was no immediate hope of bettering the situation.

Transportation by water was more expedient than by land. Unobstructed water passages extended from the ports on Lake Erie to Detroit, and thence to the posts on Lake Huron and Lake Michigan. Many rivers poured their waters into the Great Lakes, making it possible for small craft to pierce the interior of the territory. These streams provided the only avenues for the conduct of the fur trade.

Shipbuilding had been neglected during the British regime, and little progress was made after the Americans assumed control.[50] A few ships were built prior to the War of 1812, but at the outbreak of hostilities they were requisitioned for government service. While much of the shipping was destroyed during the war, the building of warships to gain control of the Lakes gave a new impetus to the industry.[51] Shipping facilities, however, were so limited that private passengers and private merchandise were refused transport in government vessels.[52] No private shipping was registered in Detroit at the close of 1814, and a year later only five ships were registered with a total capacity of 179 tons.[53] Open vessels of small draft, capable of carrying several tons, engaged in coastwise trade.[54] Ships docking in Detroit ranged in size from three to a hundred tons, but those of the latter size were rare.[55]

Transportation by water was dangerous, unreliable, and fraught with discomfort. Navigation on Lake Erie was considered more hazardous than on the Atlantic seaboard.[56] There were few good harbors—and even those were difficult to enter in swelling seas. Since its waters were shallower than those of the upper Lakes, storms were particularly severe. No lights existed to guide the ships in safe channels; often they were driven into shoal water or ran aground on sandbars.[57] Since they were subject to the capriciousness of the weather, sailing vessels found it difficult to keep a schedule. Sometimes ships arrived from Cleveland in a day and a half; at other times they required ten days.[58] The period wherein navigation was possible was of short duration. In 1815 the season opened about the middle of April, but as a rule it was considered dangerous to sail before the first of June or after the first of September.[59] Open boats, sailing close to shore, ventured between Detroit and other lake ports for a somewhat longer period.[60]

Accommodations for passengers on board the ships were very poor. Since most of the revenue was derived from carrying freight, cabin space was limited and frequently crowded. The food served was apt to be poor; one traveler found that after the second day out it consisted " wholly of yellow Ohio pork and hard peas, as soft as boiled shot." When seas were choppy the passengers suffered from sea-sickness; often so much water was shipped that their beds were soaked. Noise and confusion made sleep difficult, and after riding out a storm a boat might be becalmed for days. Frequent stops at ports along the lake added to the wearisomeness of the journey.[61] Until navigation facilities multiplied and improved, the situation of Detroit was insecure and highly vulnerable.

Overland communication between Detroit and points to the south and east was extremely difficult; transportation of supplies by land, when possible, was highly impractical. The surrender of the town during the War of 1812 was due to the lack of a suitable land route to Detroit, and its recapture was difficult and expensive for the same reason. When Great Britain held Canada and controlled the Lakes, all reenforcements and provisions for the American forces had to be sent by the land route around Lake Erie.[62] This route presented numerous difficulties, chief among which was the Black Swamp.

To reach Michigan Territory by land from the settled parts of Ohio, it was necessary to pass through this swamp. It extended along the southwestern shore of Lake Erie from Sandusky Bay to the Miami River, a distance of about forty miles, and stretched inland almost as far.[63] During the war a military road was built through it, but the road was so poorly laid out and so badly constructed that virtually all traces of it had disappeared by 1815. According to an authoritative report the road was of little use after the war, and was "principally indicated by the broken remnants of baggage wagons and gun carriages, scattered remains of flour-barrels, and the mouldering skeletons of horses and oxen remaining as they were left, just visible above the surface of the mud and wet which destroyed them." [64] After periods of rainy weather the swamp was practically impassable. One man who crossed it on foot in four days claimed that he was constantly wading in water, sometimes up to his shoulders.[65] Woodbridge hesitated for several days before attempting to cross, weighing the urgency of his mission against the expense in horse-flesh the trip would exact.[66] Blazed trees served to mark the trail, but frequently the traveler lost his way and wandered for hours in a maze of woods and bogs. Water fit for drinking was difficult

to find.[67] So completely had the war scattered the population of
the area that Ramsay Crooks declared it was " destitute of even
one solitary cabin to shelter the traveler or furnish a bit of fodder
for his famished horse." [68] Only in freezing weather could
supplies in quantity be transported through the swamp, but even
then the " teams and carriages " employed operated with " much
difficulty and expense." [69]

The horrors of the Black Swamp were widely publicized, but
it was not the only obstacle to be overcome in a journey by land
to Detroit. A veritable wilderness, level and wet and heavily
wooded, extended from the Ohio line to Detroit, and in 1815
there was no road through this expanse, nor were there any
bridges across the numerous rivers and creeks traversing it.[70]
Travelers followed narrow Indian trails that could be negotiated
on foot and, with some difficulty, on horseback; but they were
unsuited for heavy transport. An occasional trading house or
native wigwam might furnish food but seldom lodging. Other
Indian trails led north and northwest from Detroit, but since the
hinterland was uninhabited, they were traveled infrequently.[71]

When it was impossible to reach Detroit by any other route,
the traveler might attempt the journey across Upper Canada.[72]
The United States had forwarded the annuities for the Indians
living in Michigan along this route prior to the war, since it was
the only road of any kind leading to the territory.[73] It was good
in some places and bad in others, but it led through a countryside
desolated by war, wherein the rancor stirred up by the war still
smouldered.[74] During periods of rainy weather or in mild winters
this route also was impassable.[75]

The freezing weather that usually arrived in the dead of winter
provided an escape from this isolation, and French carrioles,
skimming along the ice of river and lake at a ten mile an hour
clip, could make the journey to Lower Sandusky in a day.[76]
Frequent changes in temperature, however, made this form of
communication undependable, and the carrying capacity of the

vehicles was too small to relieve the need of improved transportation facilities.[77] Perhaps the feelings of Detroiters regarding the uncertainty of land transportation were best expressed by Woodbridge when he wrote to his wife: " Since the lake navigation is opened we feel ourselves approximated some 100 miles to the inhabited parts of the globe." [78]

In addition to its inaccessibility because of uncertain water transportation and difficult land routes, the territory was almost completely detached from the rest of the country. Except for a strip of land two miles wide, all of the land between the Michigan boundary and the settlements in eastern Ohio was owned by the Indians.[79] Only the southeastern corner of the Michigan peninsula was actually owned by the United States, for the Indian title to the remainder had yet to be extinguished.[80] This government-owned land had never been surveyed and offered for sale; consequently, it was largely uninhabited, the wilderness extending to within a mile or so of Detroit. Across the river from Detroit was a foreign country which had only to gain control of the Lakes once again to make the position of the territory untenable. Thus, save for a two-mile wide boundary line with Ohio, Michigan was completely removed from contiguity with the rest of the United States.

During the war years the cost of living skyrocketed in Detroit, and in 1815 it continued to be a vexing problem. The difficulties of transport had always raised prices in Detroit to a higher level than in other regions. The war, however, had disrupted the usual trade routes between New York and Detroit, and in 1815 the facilities for receiving and trans-shipping supplies were not adequately reestablished.[81] The deficiency in vessel tonnage, combined with government priorities for military shipments, extended the period of transport and increased storage charges.[82] Following the war there was such a scarcity of merchandise in New York that the arrival of goods from England could not keep pace with the demand.[83] Consequently, the cost of imported merchandise rose sharply, and merchants having goods on hand marked them

higher. A visitor to Detroit about this time noted that the store-
keepers appeared to have a brisk trade and claimed that they
knew " how to extort an exorbitant price for every thing sold." [84]
Witherell observed that there were " many goods " in Detroit,
" yet it requires almost bills enough to cover them to purchase."
In a letter to his wife he said: " It was a fortunate circumstance
that I brought sufficient clothing with me, as anything of a single
suit would not be procured here short of $150." [85] McArthur
advised Woodbridge, before the latter set out for Detroit, that
every article for the support of a family was " extravagantly high,
and no prospect for a favorable change." When Woodbridge
arrived, he informed his wife that while he liked Detroit, he
found his prospects obscured " by the extravagantly high prices
of provisions and living." [86] In fact, during the war years, and
the years immediately following, Detroit claimed the unenviable
distinction of paying higher prices for foodstuffs than any other
market in the United States. Witherell emphasized this situation
in a letter to his wife: " I am fully persuaded that if I had a
little land to improve I could maintain the whole of our family
here cheaper than I can get myself boarded." [87]

During the war the farms on both sides of the river had been
stripped of their livestock. Consequently, the price of meat and
dairy products was excessive. To satisfy the demand for meat,
droves of cattle, sheep, and hogs were forwarded to Detroit by
the land route from southern Ohio. The army contractor sent
many head of cattle for the supply of the garrison, the Indians,
and those dependent upon the public stores for subsistence.[88] The
populace in general, however, depended upon enterprising farmers
from Ohio for their supply of meat.[89]

While small quantities of fish, cider, and fruit were exported
to Ohio at this time, the bulk of the exports from Detroit consisted of furs. Local merchants accepted them in trade, and
forwarded them to Albany or New York City to be sold. The
wholesale concerns in the East marketed the furs at a commission

rate of 2½ per cent and applied the proceeds to the merchants' accounts. They furnished responsible parties in Detroit with supplies and provisions on six-months credit, with interest at 7 per cent after that time; a discount was allowed for payments within the six-month period.[90] Since the value of the furs shipped to the seaboard was not sufficient to cover the cost of the merchandise brought to Detroit, the balances remaining had to be paid in cash.

Local manufacturing was of small consequence in 1815. This fact tended to raise living costs because it necessitated the importation of articles ordinarily produced in the home. The great majority of the populace was deficient in skill and ambition, and "with the exception of a few stockings and straw hats," turned to the merchant and his imported stock to fulfill its clothing needs. In addition to the furs they brought in, the Indians manufactured a quantity of mats, dressed deer skins, moccasins, baskets, and brooms. These articles, together with a considerable amount of maple sugar, they traded for supplies and provisions.[91]

In anticipation of large demands for goods following the war, Detroit merchants had imported large stocks from New York, and for a time business was extremely good.[92] By September, 1815, however, in consequence of the great excess of imports over exports, most of the money had been drained from the territory, and business had become "very dull."[93]

This shortage of money forced the people of Detroit to accept and extend a procedure that had evolved from the barter system. Merchants issued due bills in payment for produce or services which they redeemed in merchandise when presented for payment. These "small bills" were usually for small amounts and were issued primarily to provide a fractional currency for trade purposes. Locally, they circulated freely, but outside of the Detroit area they were of no value. In order to make payment for imported merchandise these due bills had to be converted into more negotiable currency.[94]

Prior to the War of 1812 there was a little Spanish and Portuguese gold and some French silver circulating in Detroit. By the end of 1815, however, specie had all but disappeared. That which remained was largely " cut " money, but even this rapidly disappeared in consequence of premiums offered for payment in specie.[95] Canadian residents in their dealings with citizens of Detroit made " an odds of three cents in a shilling for silver change." [96] Consequently, paper currency issued by various banks constituted the most practicable medium of exchange.

Most of the paper money in Detroit was from banks in Ohio, western Pennsylvania, and Kentucky. Public confidence in these banks fluctuated with their ability to redeem their bills in specie. The financial backing of many was open to conjecture, and their solvency was frequently questioned. Since communication was slow and difficult, and since a bill had to be presented at its source for redemption in specie, the holders of bills who were most distant from the place of issue stood the least chance of having them honored should the bank get into difficulty. As a rule, the farther west currency traveled from its source, the more it decreased in value.[97] Ohio bankpaper was discounted in Detroit at varying rates until late in 1815 when the demand for it to pay for imports became so great that it passed at par.[98]

The federal government was largely responsible for the seriousness of the currency problem in Detroit. The disbursements for the support and pay of the troops in the garrison comprised the chief source of the much-needed currency. Ordinarily, the troops were paid in Ohio money, and since there were about fifteen hundred soldiers in Detroit or its vicinity at the time, a considerable amount should have been placed in circulation.[99] At the end of 1815, however, the soldiers had not been paid for more than a year, and the curtailment of this income aggravated the money shortage and worked a hardship on the merchants. The unpaid troops were refused credit because it was feared that they might be ordered to another post before they could meet their obligations. Merchants found themselves with large stocks of goods on hand which they had purchased on credit, and no available means of paying for them.[100]

Even when business was good Detroit merchants found it difficult to make payments to their eastern creditors.[101] No bank existed to facilitate financial transactions, and exchange acceptable in the Atlantic cities was extremely difficult to obtain.[102] Ohio bank bills and drafts were subject to such large discounts in the East that merchants could ill afford to use them in payment of their imports.[103] Occasionally, they managed to purchase drafts on eastern banks or upon individuals residing in the East; sometimes they would have the good fortune to obtain British army bills which commanded a premium in New York and other eastern cities.[104] For want of an acceptable means of exchange there were times when merchants would be unable to make payments on their obligations, even though they had sufficient money on hand in the form of due bills or Ohio currency.[105]

Another factor detrimental to trade was the poor and inadequate postal service between Detroit and other parts of the United States. The schedule called for one delivery of mail each week, but since the carrier traveled by land and had to traverse the wilderness between the Ohio settlements and Detroit, it was delayed frequently.[106] So slow was the transit of mail that Cass, writing from southern Ohio, claimed: "Many a vessel has crossed the Atlantic in less time than it required to convey a letter to or from Detroit."[107] For round trip deliveries between Detroit and the East, "a full two months" was required.[108] Citizens availed themselves of every opportunity to forward letters and valuables by private conveyance, even if it was only for a part of the distance, because it was faster and more trustworthy.[109] When Woodbridge had occasion to send a message to Cass by special conveyance he forwarded one to his wife in Marietta, Ohio by the same means, for he knew it would reach her eight to ten days earlier than one he had sent her by mail two days before.[110] This slowness of communication with the East was of particular hardship to Detroit merchants, because they depended upon their New York agents for information regarding the fur market, the prices of merchandise, and the rates of exchange.[111] Such information, however, was a month old when it reached the merchants. Consequently, they were forced to gamble on the stability of the markets in all their commercial transactions, and with furs especially, if they were not kept informed of price fluctuations, they might make purchases at rates which would prove ruinous.[112]

Difficult as were all of the handicaps under which the people of Detroit labored, there was small prospect of any immediate relief. The war had made the area better known throughout the nation than it had ever been before, but it had also demonstrated the inherent weakness of the region. In spite of the fact that Witherell noted there was "a great influx of people to this vicinity, some purchasing farms, some bringing goods, etc.," and the area seemed "to be verging more to Americans," there was little to attract settlers in large numbers.[113] The *habitants* clung to their unimproved farms, and the public lands were yet to be surveyed and offered for sale; consequently, those arriving in the territory with the intention of settling found it extremely difficult to obtain land. The lack of knowledge concerning the hinterland was a contributing factor to the slow development of the region. Many of the Americans who had gathered in Detroit following the war were told that the land north of the post was so swampy that it was unfit for agriculture and left to seek homes elsewhere.[114] Not even the lands in the Ten Thousand Acre Tract, which had been given to the town of Detroit by the federal government following the fire of 1805, could be sold, for all the records of boundaries and sales had been carried away or destroyed by the British.[115] With so little to offer the prospective settler, the Detroit area could not anticipate a great increase in population.

In 1815 there was small means to acquaint the federal government with the state of affairs in Detroit and Michigan Territory.

There was no newspaper to come to the defense of the area and to point out the seriousness of the problems it faced. Since Michigan was a territory of the " first grade," it was not entitled to a representative in Congress. In fact, no congressman lived within two hundred miles of Michigan.[116] Thus there was no voice in the national legislature to demand aid for the inhabitants of the territory and to introduce measures for reform. The majority of the people were uneducated and illiterate, skeptical of American ways and American institutions, and, therefore, incapable of articulate exertions in their own behalf.

Following the American reoccupation of Michigan the rule of the Governor and Judges was reinstated. Cass, as Governor, sincerely desired to bring about reconstruction of the territory and to relieve it of its major problems.[117] He felt that it would take many years to accomplish the task, for, as he wrote to Woodbridge, " there is little probability of a state being established there [Michigan] during your day or mine." [118] He endeavored to alleviate the discontent of the populace of Detroit in regard to the return of the autocratic government of the Governor and Judges by providing for a more democratic form of local government. He and the Judges passed a bill which reincorporated the town of Detroit as the city of Detroit. The new charter provided for a local government to be administered by a Board of Trustees, five in number, elected annually by the qualified voters of the city.[119]

Thus Detroit became a city—an American city with a French people in the majority; a frontier city, virtually isolated from the rest of the nation by turbulent waters and an unbroken wilderness; a city ravaged by war and stricken by poverty, dependent for its very existence upon the gratuities and expenditures of a paternal administration; a city in which " everything seemed to be entirely unhinged," [120] with small hope for a brighter future. The manner in which Detroit met its varied problems in the first decade of its history as a city will be treated in the following chapters.

CHAPTER I—NOTES

[1] A facsimile of the Articles of Capitulation is in Silas Farmer, *History of Detroit and Michigan, or, The Metropolis Illustrated; A Chronological Cyclopaedia of the Past and Present* . . . (Detroit, 1884), p. 278.

[2] *Ibid.*, pp. 284-285; Lewis Cass to James Monroe, September 30, 1814, Clarence Edwin Carter, ed. and comp., *Territorial Papers of the United States* (10 vols.; Washington, 1934-42), X, 486-89.

[3] Although the Treaty of Ghent was signed December 24, 1814, the news of peace did not reach Detroit until about February 20, 1815.—Colonel Anthony Butler to William Woodbridge, February 20, 1815, "Woodbridge Papers" (MS, Burton Historical Collection, Detroit Public Library, Detroit; hereafter cited as B. H. C.).

[4] Lewis Cass, Henry R. Schoolcraft, Henry Whiting, and John Biddle, *Historical and Scientific Sketches of Michigan, Comprising a Series of Discourses Delivered before the Historical Society of Michigan, and Other Interesting Papers Relative to the Territory* (Detroit, 1834), pp. 137-38.

[5] Cass to Woodbridge, November 9, 1813, "Woodbridge Papers."

[6] Judge Augustus B. Woodward to James Monroe, March 5, 1815, Carter, *op. cit.*, X, 513-14; *Detroit Gazette*, March 10, 1820.

[7] *Detroit Gazette*, March 10, 1820, October 25, 1822. See also Cass to Robert Brent, September 20, 1814, "Cass Papers" (MS, B. H. C.).

[8] For a list of those exiled from Detroit see *Niles' Weekly Register*, November 6, 1813. See also Richard Smyth to Joriah Brady, March 20, 1813, "Joriah Brady Papers" (MS, B. H. C.); George McDougall to Woodward, February 2, 1813, "Augustus Woodward Papers" (MS, B. H. C.); Woodward to Monroe, March 22, 1813, Carter, *op. cit.*, X, 436. The original of a notification ordering H. J. B. Brevort and William Macomb to leave the country, dated February 1, 1813, is in the "B. F. H. Witherell Papers" (MS, B. H. C.).

[9] *Detroit Gazette*, March 10, 1820.

[10] Facsimiles of General Henry Proctor's proclamations providing for civil law and martial law are in Farmer, *op. cit.*, p. 279. See also the original of a proclamation of martial law in "Witherell Papers," September 13, 1813.

[11] "The war has produced a great relaxation of morals in this place."—Solomon Sibley to Reverend Backus, [spring (?)] 1815. "Solomon Sibley Papers" (MS, B. H. C.).

[12] Farmer, *op. cit.*, pp. 283-84; Woodbridge to James Monroe, February 5, 1815, Woodbridge to his wife, March 28, 1815, "Woodbridge Papers"; Clarence M. Burton, comp., and M. Agnes Burton, ed., *Governor and Judges Journal, Proceedings of the Land Board of Detroit* ([Detroit], 1915), pp. 58-59.

[13] Cass to Woodbridge, November 9, 1813, "Woodbridge Papers."

[14] James McCloskey's agreement to appoint appraisers to determine the damages to the Springwells property of John R. Williams, June 26, 1815, "John R. Williams Papers ' (MS, B. H. C.). See also "John R. Williams Letterbook, 1815-1825 " (MS, property of Frederick Douglas, Denver, Colorado).

[15] B. O. Williams, "Early Michigan, Sketch of the Life of Oliver Williams and Family," *Michigan Pioneer and Historical Society, Collections* (40 vols.; Lansing, 1877-1929), II, 38. (Hereafter cited as *M. P. H. S., C.*). See also Cass to William H. Crawford, May 31, 1816, Carter, *op. cit.*, X, 642. Samuel R. Brown, who

visited Detroit in 1814, reported: "The population is three fourths of French extraction, and very few understand any other language."—Samuel R. Brown, *Views on Lake Erie* (Troy, 1814), p. 95. The *Detroit Gazette*, January 29, 1819, claimed that no exact census of the city was taken until 1819.

¹⁶ Woodbridge to Thomas Worthington, February 25, 1815, "Woodbridge Papers."

¹⁷ Woodbridge to Monroe, March 18, 1815, *M. P. H. S., C.*, XXXVI, 318.

¹⁸ March 6, 1815, "Woodbridge Papers."

¹⁹ Woodward to Monroe, March 5, 1815, Carter, *op. cit.*, X, 513-14.

²⁰ Cass to Woodbridge, March 23, 1815, "Woodbridge Papers."

²¹ A. J. Dallas to Cass, May 25, 1815, Carter, *op. cit.*, X, 541-42.

²² Cass to Dallas, July 22, 1815, *M. P. H. S., C.*, XXXVI, 383.

²³ *Ibid.*, 383-84.

²⁴ George Graham to Cass, August 30, 1815, Carter, *op. cit.*, X, 593.

²⁵ Cass, "Regulations for the Administration of Relief," dated September 23, 1815, Carter, *op. cit.*, X, 645-46; Cass, "Circular to the Justices of the Peace," September 23, 1815, "A. D. Fraser Papers" (MS, B. H. C.).

²⁶ James Witherell to his wife, October 14, 1815, "Witherell Papers."

²⁷ George N. Fuller, "An Introduction to the Settlement of Southern Michigan, 1815-1835," *M. P. H. S., C.*, XXXVIII, 540; Isaac Weld, Jr., *Travels Through the States of North America and the Provinces of Upper Canada During the Years 1795, 1796, and 1797* (London, 1799), p. 532.

²⁸ Cass to Crawford, May 21, 1816, Carter, *op. cit.*, X, 642-43; C. F. Volney, *A View of the Soil and Climate of the United States of America*, C. B. Brown, trans. (Philadelphia, 1804), pp. 336-37.

²⁹ *American State Papers* . . . (38 vols.; Washington, 1832-1861), *Miscellaneous*, I, 461.

³⁰ See Article III, "Treaty of Amity, Commerce and Navigation. Concluded November 19, 1794; Ratification exchanged at London October 28, 1795; Proclaimed February 29, 1796," in *Treatises and Conventions Between the United States and Other Powers Since July 4, 1776* (Washington, 1889), p. 380.

³¹ Josiah Dunham to William Clark, August 20, 1807; Francis Le Baron to Henry Dearborn, March 20, 1809; Cass to Dallas, July 20, 1815; Cass to Crawford, May 31, 1816, Carter, *op. cit.*, X, 127-29, 271-72, 574, 642-43.

³² Brown, *op. cit.*, pp. 94-95.

³³ Duncan McArthur to James Monroe, February 6, 1815, Carter, *op. cit.*, X, 503.

³⁴ Farmer, *op. cit.*, p. 13.

³⁵ Thomas J. Drake, "History of Oakland County," *M. P. H. S., C.*, III, 566.

³⁶ On this paragraph see *Detroit Gazette*, October 3, 1817, November 7, 1817, January 22, 1819, July 30, 1819, November 5, 1819; Cass to Crawford, May 31, 186, Carter, *op. cit.*, X, 642-43; Woodbridge to his wife, April 7, 1815, "Woodbridge Papers"; Elkanah Watson, *Men and Times of the Revolution, or Memoirs of Elkanah Watson, Including Journals of Travels in Europe and America,* . . . Winslow C. Watson, ed. (New York, 1856), pp. 428, 430; *American State Papers, Miscellaneous*, I, 461.

³⁷ James D. Richardson, comp., *A Compilation of the Messages and Papers of the Presidents* (rev. ed., 11 vols.; n. p., 1913), I, 522; John Armstrong to Cass, June 11, 18, 1814, Cass and William Henry Harrison to Armstrong, July 25, 1814, Carter, *op. cit.*, X, 462-63, 465-66.

[38] Cass, Schoolcraft, Whiting, and Biddle, *op. cit.*, p. 144.

[39] Witherell to his wife, September 25, 1814, " Witherell Papers "; *Niles' Weekly Register*, November 19, 1814.

[40] Brown, *op. cit.*, p. 95; Richardson, *op. cit.*, I, 527; Woodbridge to his wife, January 16-18, 1815, " Woodbridge Papers."

[41] Cass to Woodbridge, November 9, 1813, Woodbridge to Worthington, February 25, 1815, " Woodbridge Papers "; Cass to Monroe, September 15, 1814, Carter, *op. cit.*, X, 484-85.

[42] " I have seen the women and children [Indians] searching about the ground for bones and rinds of pork, which had been thrown away by the soldiers; meat in a high state of putrefaction, which had been thrown into the river, was carefully picked up and devoured; the feet, heads and entrails of the cattle slaughtered by the public butchers, were collected and sent off to the neighboring villages. I have counted twenty horses in a drove fancifully decorated with the offals of the slaughter-yard."—Brown, *op. cit.*, p. 95.

[43] Butler to Woodbridge, February 20, 1815, Woodbridge to his wife, January 16-18, 1815, Woodbridge to Worthington, February 25, 1815, " Woodbridge Papers "; Woodbridge to Monroe, January 26, February 11, 1815, Carter, *op. cit.*, X, 500-03, 505-07.

[44] Butler to Woodbridge, February 20, 1815, " Woodbridge Papers."

[45] February 17, 1816, " Witherell Papers."

[46] *Detroit Gazette*, July 25, November 21, 1817, July 30, August 13, 1819; Watson, *op. cit.*, p. 429; Estwick Evans, " Evans' Pedestrious Tour of Four Thousand Miles—1818," in Reuben Gold Thwaites, ed., *Early Western Travels, 1748-1846* (32 vols.; Cleveland, 1904), VIII, 219, 222.

[47] McArthur to Monroe, December 10, 1814, Carter, *op. cit.*, X, 497.

[48] Butler to Woodbridge, April 10, 1815, " Woodbridge Papers." A few days before this Butler had used his authority as military commandant to requisition the ships for military use, regardless of customs office formalities. He did not wish the situation to continue, however, because he did not believe it was a military matter.—Butler to Woodbridge, March 30, 1815, " Woodbridge Papers."

[49] United States Custom House, Detroit, William Woodbridge, Collector, " Impost Book " (MS, B. H. C.), pp. 3-4.

[50] The British government had discouraged the building of private vessels, fearing that they might be employed in smuggling. All private merchandise had to be carried in government ships, or in private ships escorted by them.—General Frederick Haldiman, memorandum to Lord Sydney, *circa* 1786, *M. P. H. S., C.*, XX, 279. See also " Petition Relative to Vessels " and the statement of William Robertson before the committee appointed by Lord Dorchester to consider a memorial of the inhabitants of Detroit, *M. P. H. S., C.*, XI, 424, 641.

[51] Almon Ernest Parkins, *The Historical Geography of Detroit* (Lansing, 1918), pp. 215-16, 224.

[52] Ramsay Crooks to John Jacob Astor, October 31, 1813, May 8, 1814, " Ramsay Crooks Papers " (Photostat, MS, B. H. C.). See also Williams to Boyd & Suydam, December 30, 1815, " Williams Letterbook."

[53] United States Custom House, Detroit, William Woodbridge, Collector, " Vessel Register, Detroit, 1815-1824 " (MS, B. H. C.), p. 1; *American State Papers, Commerce and Navigation*, II, 14-15. This latter source, p. 41, shows 159 tons of shipping registered at Detroit at the end of the year 1815.

[54] United States Custom House, Detroit, William Woodbridge, Collector, " Day-

book, 1815-1828 " (MS, 11 vols.; B. H. C., no pagination), I, April 4, 5, 9, 20, May 3, 9, 13, 1815.

[55] Woodbridge to his wife, April 30, 1815, "Woodbridge Papers"; Clarence M. Burton, *History of Detroit 1780-1850, Financial and Commercial* (Detroit, 1917), p. 97.

[56] William Darby, *A Tour from the City of New York to Detroit in Michigan Territory, made between the 2nd of May and 22nd of September, 1818* (New York, 1819), p. 207; *American State Papers, Miscellaneous*, II, 596.

[57] Darby, *op. cit.*, p. 207; Watson, *op. cit.*, p. 427.

[58] Woodbridge to his wife, April 30, 1815, "Woodbridge Papers."

[59] *Ibid.*; Charles C. Trowbridge, "Detroit Past and Present in Relation to its Social and Physical Condition," *M. P. H. S., C.*, I, 383.

[60] United States Custom House, "Daybook," I, December, 1815, and April, 1816, *passim*.

[61] Watson colorfully described the rigors of a journey to Detroit on the sailing vessel *Franklin*, June 23-July 2, 1818. He walked the last two miles to Detroit.— Watson, *op. cit.*, pp. 420-26. Witherell sailed from Detroit on November 5, 1814, arriving at Presque Isle (Erie, Pennsylvania), 240 miles from Detroit, on November 14. The ship encountered "some calms—some storms, etc." On his return trip the next year he waited some time at Buffalo to get passage on a vessel to Detroit. After he secured a berth, a gale delayed the departure of the ship for several days, and after leaving port it ran into another storm and was grounded on a sandbar. During the confusion Witherell fell overboard, was rescued, rode in a wagon to Cleveland, and along with some others chartered a ship to continue the journey to Detroit. This ship sprung a leak and was purposely beached on an island, where the passengers were marooned for several days without food. Finally, he managed to reach the Canadian shore, and in a few days reached his destination. A month had passed since he left Buffalo.—Witherell to his wife, November 14, 1814, and September 29, 1815, "Witherell Papers."

[62] G. B. Catlin, "The Black Swamp," "G. B. Catlin Papers" (MS, B. H. C.); Harrison and John Graham to Dallas, July 14, 1815, Carter, *op. cit.*, X, 571.

[63] A. N. Bliss, "Land Grants for Internal Improvements," *M. P. H. S., C.*, VII, 53.

[64] *American State Papers, Miscellaneous*, II, 593.

[65] Evans, *op. cit.*, pp. 200-04; Benjamin Hough to Edward Tiffin, May 20, 1815, Carter, *op. cit.*, X, 540.

[66] Woodbridge to his wife, January 12, 16-18, 1815, "Woodbridge Papers."

[67] Tilly Buttrick, Jr., "Buttrick's Voyages, Travels, and Discoveries 1812-1819," in Thwaites, *op. cit.*, VIII, 83.

[68] Crooks to Astor, December 1, 1813, "Ramsay Crooks Papers."

[69] McArthur to Monroe, December 10, 1814, Carter, *op. cit.*, X, 497.

[70] *American State Papers, Miscellaneous*, II, 596. Evans claimed that within one hundred miles of Detroit—south and east—he had forded upwards of thirty rivers and creeks.—Evans, *op. cit.*, p. 215.

[71] James V. Campbell, "Sketches of Charles C. Trowbridge," *M. P. H. S., C.*, VI, 484.

[72] Bliss, *op. cit.*, p. 53.

[73] *American State Papers, Miscellaneous*, II, 593.

[74] Brown, *op. cit.*, pp. 55, 65.

[75] John R. Williams was forced to spend the entire winter of 1805-1806 at

Niagara, for he missed the last boat out of Fort Erie for Detroit in the fall, and
the winter was so mild that it was impossible to travel overland because of the
softness of the roads.—Williams to J. T. Duryee, March 3, 1806, "Williams
Papers."

⁷⁶ Woodbridge to his wife, February 2, 1815, and January 27, 1816, "Woodbridge
Papers."

⁷⁷ Witherell to his wife, October 29, 1815, "Witherell Papers."

⁷⁸ April 30, 1815, "Woodbridge Papers."

⁷⁹ *American State Papers, Miscellaneous,* II, 593, 596.

⁸⁰ For a map showing the various Indian land cessions in the Lower Peninsula of
Michigan between 1795 and 1837, together with descriptions of the cessions, see
George N. Fuller, *Economic and Social Beginnings of Michigan, A Study of the
Settlement of the Lower Peninsula During the Territorial Period, 1805-1837*
(Lansing, 1916), pp. lxiv, 520-30.

⁸¹ James Kirby to Williams, April 8, 1815, "Williams Papers."

⁸² Williams to Boyd & Suydam, December 30, 1850, June 1, 1816, "Williams
Letterbook."

⁸³ Robert Gill and Company to Williams, August 25, 1815, "Williams Papers."

⁸⁴ Brown, *op. cit.,* pp. 94-95.

⁸⁵ September 4, 25, 1814, "Witherell Papers."

⁸⁶ McArthur to Woodbridge, November 17, 1814, Woodbridge to his wife,
January 11-18, 25, 1815, "Woodbridge Papers."

⁸⁷ October 14, 1815, "Witherell Papers."

⁸⁸ According to McArthur the contractor had agreed to deliver "seventy thousand
rations of flour, meat and salt . . . at Detroit on or before the 20th of August,"
1815. These provisions were to be sent from Ohio.—McArthur to Graham, July
18, 1815, Carter, *op. cit.,* X, 572. See also John Piatt to Armstrong, June 4, 1814,
Carter, *op. cit.,* X, 461-62.

⁸⁹ Williams to Boyd & Suydam, September 23, 1815, "Williams Letterbook."
While no definite figures have been found to illustrate the extent of these importations, custom house records indicate that much livestock was exported from Detroit
to Canada by citizens of Ohio.—United States Custom House, "Daybook," I,
passim.

⁹⁰ *Detroit Gazette,* November 21, 1817, July 30 and August 13, 1819; Williams
to Cummings & Day, May 11, 1810, Starr & Smith to Williams, November 20,
1815, Boyd & Suydam to Williams, October 7, 1815, October 18, 1820, "Williams
Papers"; Williams to David Boyd & Co., July 15, 23, 1815, Williams to Boyd &
Suydam, July 15, 1815, "Williams Letterbook."

⁹¹ *Detroit Gazette,* July 30, 1819; Cass to Crawford, May 31, 1816, Carter,
op. cit., X, 642-43.

⁹² This happened throughout the region. "There never was so much business
done in this place [New York City] as in the last year—The western country
is now completely glutted with goods, and many failures are look'd for in that
quarter."—Boyd & Suydam to Williams, January 5, 1816, "Williams Papers";
Williams to Boyd & Suydam, July 15, 29, 1815, "Williams Letterbook."

⁹³ Williams to Boyd & Suydam, September 23, 1815, "Williams Letterbook."

⁹⁴ Williams to Boyd & Suydam, September 23, December 30, 1815, "Williams
Letterbook"; *Detroit Gazette,* September 5, 12, 1817; Trowbridge, *op. cit.,* p. 382.

⁹⁵ Silver dollars and half-dollars were cut into triangular pieces to provide

fractional change. Sometimes, however, a dollar would be cut into nine or ten equal parts instead of eight, and each piece passed as a " York shilling," equivalent to twelve and a half cents. The difficulty of distinguishing between an eighth part and a ninth or tenth part of a dollar enabled dishonest characters to realize a profit by cutting up specie.—Trowbridge, *op. cit.*, pp. 381-82; B. O. Williams, *op. cit.*, p. 38.

[96] *Detroit Gazette*, October 10, 1817.

[97] Cass to John C. Calhoun, October 17, 1821, United States House of Representatives, *House Doc. No. 60, 17th Congress, 1st Session* (Washington, 1822), pp. 113-14; Henry Bradshaw Fearon, *Sketches of America* (London, 1819), pp. 232-33; David Boyd to Williams, October 14, 1815, " Williams Papers "; Farmer, *op. cit.*, p. 847.

[98] Williams to Boyd & Suydam, September 23, 1815, " Williams Letterbook."

[99] Witherell to his wife, October 14, 1815, " Witherell Papers "; *Niles' Weekly Register*, January 18, 1817; General Alexander Macomb to Robert Brent, November 10, 1816, " Alexander Macomb Letterbook, 1807-1819 " (Typescript, B. H.C.).

[100] Williams to Boyd & Suydam, September 23, December 30, 1815, " Williams Letterbook.'

[101] Williams to Boyd & Suydam, July 15, 1815, " Williams Letterbook."

[102] " As to money you must do as well as you can. There is none here which would pass there if I should send it."—Witherell to his wife, January 20, 1816, " Witherell Papers."

[103] Boyd & Suydam to Williams, July 26, 1815, May 23, 1816, " Williams Papers."

[104] Williams to Boyd & Suydam, August 3 , 1815, " Williams Letterbook "; Boyd & Suydam to Williams, October 7, 1815, " Williams Papers."

[105] Williams to Boyd & Suydam, August 3, 1815, March 9, 1816, " Williams Letterbook."

[106] Cass to Woodbridge, February 14, 1815, " Woodbridge Papers "; *Detroit Gazette*, September 12, 19, 1817; R. J. Meigs to Woodbridge, April 6, 1815, Meigs to Cass, February 10, 1816, Meigs to Ashbel W. Walworth, February 10, 1816, Carter, *op. cit.*, X, 526, 622.

[107] Cass to Woodbridge, February 14, 1815, " Woodbridge Papers."

[108] Witherell advised his wife in Vermont that if he was to receive her letter in Detroit by the first of June, she would have to mail it by the first of May.—Witherell to his wife, February 17, and March 25, 1816, " Witherell Papers."

[109] Sibley asked Governor Worthington of Ohio to send certain valuable papers " by some safe hand bound for Detroit and not by mail."—Sibley to Worthington, July 20, 1815, " Sibley Papers." " I should not trouble you so soon with another letter (having written you on the 5th inst.) were it not that this will go by a water passage, and from Buffalo to Albany by a private hand."—Witherell to his wife, November 9, 1815, " Witherell Papers." On the margins of certain letters forwarded to his creditors in New York, Williams inscribed " pr. Desnoyers," i. e., in care of Mr. Desnoyers. Later in the year he sent a letter containing $800.00 to a creditor " by Colo. Jenkins."—Williams to David J. Boyd & Co., July 14, 1815, Williams to Boyd & Suydam, July 15, September 23, 1815, " Williams Letterbook."

[110] Woodbridge to his wife, March 7, 1815, " Woodbridge Papers."

[111] Boyd & Suydam to Williams, October 7, 1815, January 5, 1816, " Williams Papers "; Williams to David J. Boyd & Co., July 23, 1815, " Williams Letterbook."

[112] Williams to David J. Boyd & Co., July 23, 1815, Williams to Boyd & Suydam, May 3, 1817, " Williams Letterbook."

[113] Witherell to his wife, November 9, 1815, February 17, 1816, " Witherell Papers."

[114] Cass to Josiah Meigs, May 11, 1816 (two letters), Meigs to James Abbott, May 30, 1816, Cass to Crawford, May 31, 1816, Abbott to Meigs, June 30, 1816, Carter, *op. cit.*, X, 633-36, 641, 643, 655-57; Drake, *op. cit.*, p. 565.

[115] Burton and Burton, *op. cit.*, pp. 58-59; Cass to Edward Tiffin, January 26, 1816, Carter, *op. cit.*, X, 618.

[116] *Detroit Gazette*, October 2, 1818.

[117] Cass to Dallas, July 22, 1815, *M. P. H. S., C.*, XXXVI, 383-84; Cass to Crawford, May 31, 1816, Carter, *op. cit.*, X, 642-45.

[118] Cass to Woodbridge, October 21, 1814, " Woodbridge Papers."

[119] *Laws of the Territory of Michigan* (4 vols.; Lansing, 1871), I, 534-41. For a digest of this charter see George B. Catlin, " Digest of the Act of Incorporation of the Town of Detroit on October 24, 1815, and also a Digest of the Proceedings of the Board of Trustees Adopted by the Board of the Governor & Judges of the Northwest Territory to September 6, 1824 " (Typescript, B. H. C.).

[120] Williams to David J. Boyd & Co., July 23, 1815, " Williams Letterbook."

CHAPTER II

Transportation and Communication

In 1815 the area bordering the Great Lakes constituted the north-western frontier of the United States. Most of the inhabitants of Ohio had followed the natural highway offered by the Ohio River and had settled along its banks and those of its tributaries. Thus they had relatively cheap communication with the sources of supply at Pittsburgh, and a choice of either Pittsburgh or New Orleans as a market for their produce. Ohio was admitted as a state as early as 1803. In 1815 its attractiveness for the prospective emigrant was enhanced by the appearance of steamboats on the Ohio and the Mississippi. Colonel Anthony Butler, former commandant at Detroit, having returned to Kentucky after the war, wrote to Solomon Sibley urging him to move to the Ohio region in order to benefit by its increased advantages:

> The business of this country has received a very great spring by the adoption and success of the steam boat navigation—it opens to the western states an avenue through which the whole resources they possess may be put into activity, and by lessening so greatly the expense and difficulty attending the transportation of our bulky articles of produce, gives to us the advantage over all the rest of the Union— This proposition is clear to demonstration—for the expense of

carriage now to Orleans and from Orleans is less than from
the interior of Pennsylvania, New York, or Maryland to their
seaboard— Add to that circumstance the consideration of a
soil fertile to abundance and a climate in which health is
characteristic, and you see at once the basis upon which the
conclusion rests.[1]

Easterners desirous of removing to the western country were
reluctant to settle in an area devoid of such advantages, and,
consequently, following the War of 1812 the great influx of
settlers was along the line of the earlier infiltrations. As late as
1820 the southern shore lands of Lake Erie had a population
of only six to eighteen persons per square mile, and those at the
southwestern and western ends only two to six per square mile.[2]
Although these lands were known to be fertile and the climate
mild, they could attract no agricultural population of consequence
until transportation costs lessened and facilities improved. Transportation to either eastern or southern markets from the Lake
Erie area involved land carriage, and since it was estimated that
transport of a mile by land was equivalent in cost to twenty miles
by water, a farmer of the lake region could not possibly compete
with one in a more favored locality.[3] In 1817 a contributor to
the *Niles' Weekly Register* commented in this regard as follows:

> From the lakes, the export trade, except in furs and peltry,
> is inconsiderable, because there is no channel through which
> the productions of the country can be conveyed to market.
> The cataract of Niagara presents an insuperable obstacle
> to the navigation between the upper lakes and Lake Ontario,
> and even from the latter, the only outlet to the ocean (the
> St. Lawrence) passes through the dominions of a foreign
> country.[4]

Furs and peltries, together with other products indigenous to the
Detroit area, such as maple sugar, fish, and cider, could be transported profitably to eastern and southern markets. This was

possible because they represented large value in comparatively small bulk, or because they could be obtained from no other quarter.

The improvements in transportation and communication between Detroit and the East which took place in the decade following the war were both a cause and a result of the increase in population and the development of industry. Since it was more feasible than transportation by land, the greatest improvements occurred in the facilities for transportation by water.

Until the year 1818 no changes in the status of the lake country were sufficiently revolutionary to make it more desirable for the prospective immigrant. Neither were there any noteworthy advances in water transportation, except for an increase in the number of ships engaged in trade and passenger service. At the close of 1815 only 828 tons of shipping were registered at the various Lake Erie ports, and most of it was chartered by the federal government and employed in transporting supplies for the troops at the several military posts on the Lakes.[5] Private freight was refused transit until late in the season, but early winter storms then took a heavy toll of both ships and cargoes.[6] So few were the ships and so heavy the military requirements that it was difficult to obtain passenger service from Buffalo to Detroit.[7] Beginning in 1816, however, lake commerce assumed the proportions of pre-war years, and with the growth of trade, new vessels appeared upon the waters.[8] By 1818 there were fifty ships on Lake Erie ranging in size from 10 to 132 tons, with a total capacity of 1,859 tons. Vessels under 10 tons, plus the estimated tonnage of vessels omitted or unknown, amounted to 211 tons. There were seven ships of 70 tons or more engaged in the lake trade, all of which were registered at either Buffalo or Presque Isle. The schooners *Jackson* and *Hercules* were the largest vessels plying out of Detroit, both being of about 60 tons burden.[9] Fourteen of the fifty vessels of more than 10 tons were included in the 633 tons of shipping registered at Detroit.[10]

The ships belonging to the districts of Buffalo, Presque Isle, and Detroit were employed, principally, in transporting merchandise from Buffalo to Detroit, Mackinac, and the posts on Lake Michigan. Those owned at Cleveland and Sandusky were active in forwarding foodstuffs from Ohio to Detroit, as well as to the military posts on the upper Lakes. On their return voyages the ships usually carried fish, furs, cider, and apples.[11]

Some Detroit merchants continued to purchase their goods for the Indian trade in Montreal.[12] It was deemed more convenient to transport this merchandise in open boats such as piroques, bateaux, canoes, and durham boats than in larger vessels.[13] Their light draft enabled them to penetrate the River Thames to its head, and there take on goods wagoned from the western end of Lake Ontario.[14] Practically all foreign goods arriving in Sandwich for Detroit use was shipped across the river in canoe or open boat.[15] Occasionally, an open boat would make the complete journey from Montreal, probably portaging by wagon around Niagara Falls, and hugging the northern shore of Lake Erie until it reached Detroit.[16]

Open boats of the various types were of prime importance in transporting supplies to Detroit from other lake ports. The dreaded storms of Lake Erie had less effect upon them than upon ships of greater draft. Every small river or creek was a haven to ride out a storm; or, if necessary, the boat could be beached with small harm to ship or cargo. The large Indian canoe, constructed of birch or elm bark, could carry up to four tons of freight and a crew of from six to eight men. It was well adapted to inland transportation because of its light weight and the ease with which it could be portaged, and was used extensively by the great fur companies.[17] The canoes used in the Detroit area were undoubtedly of smaller size, probably seldom having a capacity of more than two tons.[18] They were employed in ferry service between Detroit and Sandwich, and French farmers used them to commute to the city.[19] They were used sparingly for lake transit, for they were

easily damaged on shallow, stony beaches; besides, their comparatively small capacity tended to increase transportation costs.[20]
By 1815, in the Detroit area, they had been largely superseded
by more substantial types of craft.

The piroque, bateau, and durham boat were better suited for
lake transportation. The piroque was a large wooden canoe,
" capable of holding three or four passengers and a crew of half
a dozen men, with their baggage." [21] In 1816 a piroque carried
150 bushels of corn from Detroit to Sandwich.[22] This type of
boat was constructed by hollowing out a tree, splitting it length-
wise, and using the halves for siding; planks then were inserted
in the bottom and ends.[23] It was used extensively in the fur
trade between Detroit and the Maumee River region. In the spring
of the year piroques would arrive in Detroit with furs from the
Fort Wayne (Indiana) area, and in the late summer or fall
would return with Indian trade goods.[24]

The bateau was constructed wholly of hewn timber. It had
straight sides up and down, and was pointed at both ends. It
would be propelled with oars in deep water but most frequently,
when loaded, followed the shorelines closely, its crew pushing
it forward through the shallow water by means of metal-tipped
setting poles. Sometimes it was equipped with a sail to take
advantage of favorable winds. The crew of as many as five men
camped on shore at night; sometimes they would walk along the
shore towing the boat with lines. The bateaux were built in
various sizes, the largest being from three to four tons burden.
During the British regime they constituted an important means
of transport between Niagara and Detroit.[25] In 1816 they were in
use between Detroit and the Maumee River region, and probably
traveled as far as Cleveland.[26] The advent of the durham boat
and the increase in the number of sailing vessels gradually
rendered transportation by bateaux unprofitable.[27]

Introduced on the Lakes by the American forces during the War
of 1812, the durham boat was a heavy freight craft, the lines of

which resembled those of an Indian canoe. Ordinarily, it was sixty feet long, eight feet wide, and two feet deep; when loaded with fifteen tons of freight it drew but twenty inches of water.[28] It was flat-bottomed, had a keel and centerboard; and was rounded at both ends, with a deck at bow and stern. A wide gunwale extended the whole length on both sides, upon which the crew trod when poling the boat. The crew towed the vessel through swift water and when the wind was favorable used sails.[29] Many of the arrivals and clearances of the " open boats " noted in the records of the Custom House in Detroit may have referred to durham boats, although they were not so termed. These boats carried cargoes to Detroit from Miami (Toledo), Cuyahoga (Cleveland), Presque Isle (Erie), and Buffalo Creek (Buffalo). Frequently, for want of cargo, they would return to their home ports " in ballast," or with a few passengers.[30] These boats were also of various sizes; one recorded as clearing for Cuyahoga was " about 5 tons," while another was capable of carrying eighty barrels of salt. The owner of a lost boat advertised in the *Detroit Gazette* that it was " between 50 and 55 feet long." [31]

While sailing vessels were scarce on the Lakes, open craft of the various types fulfilled a definite need. Undoubtedly, the threat of starvation at Detroit would have been more serious if the people had been forced to rely solely upon sailing craft to bring produce from Ohio.[32] Merchants and producers preferred to forward their goods in sloops and schooners, because they offered safer and cheaper transportation; and as these increased in number, the importance of open boats in the carrying trade diminished. With the appearance of steamboats on the Lakes, it was further reduced. In 1825 regular steamboat packet service was introduced between Detroit and Sandusky, the trade route once most favorable for the open boats.[33]

Transportation by sailing vessel was dangerous and undependable, but offered the best means of communication with the East until the arrival of the steamboat. As the lake area increased in population, the number of vessels in service multiplied. Passenger fare between Detroit and Buffalo in 1817 was $15.00, and the *Gazette* claimed that from May 10th to November 10th of that year $15,000 had been paid to ship owners in fares alone.[34] Subsequently, an increase in the number of passengers and in steamboat competition served to reduce the fare. Sailing time by schooner between Detroit and Buffalo was approximately two weeks, but frequently, contrary winds delayed the departure of vessels or lengthened the time of the voyage;[35] and, as already indicated in Chapter I, the dangers and discomfitures attending a voyage were many, for storms were common and few provisions were offered for passenger comfort. In 1817 the editor of the *Gazette* believed that hundreds were deterred from visiting Detroit " in consequence of the uncertainty of having a quick and pleasant voyage in schooners."[36] Nevertheless, during the years that followed, thousands of easterners loaded their families and household goods into small sailing vessels and set out to found new homes in Michigan and other parts of the Northwest Territory. On May 6, 1822, according to the *Gazette*, " Nine fine schooners . . . aided by a favorable wind, could be seen bearing into port with all their sails set. They were from Buffalo, and other ports on Lake Erie. . . . By the arrival of the vessels at this port our territory has received a valuable acquisition in emigrants."[37] A month later the paper claimed that " almost every vessel which has touched at this port, has brought emigrants."[38] The schooner *Huntington* landed 74 passengers at Detroit in 1823, " nearly all emigrants," and in 1825 the *Good Intent* brought 45. The schooner *Superior* left Buffalo in April of that year " with 160 emigrants all for Michigan," and the schooners *Huntington, Lake Serpent*, and *Neptune* arrived a fortnight later " crowded with emigrants."[39] These notices indicate that by 1825 a major portion of schooner cargo westward consisted of passengers and household goods.

Schooners carried most of the freight on the Lakes until steamboat tonnage began to increase about 1825. Cargoes shipped westward far exceeded in bulk those shipped to the East. From Buffalo and other Lake Erie ports a great variety of merchandise and provisions departed in schooners to supply the needs of the inhabitants and the garrisons at Detroit and the posts on the upper Lakes.[40] This trade continued even after Michigan Territory became comparatively populous, for settlers arrived in such numbers that local production could not satisfy their demands.[41] Despite the deficiency in freight eastward, some of the cargoes entrusted to schooner transport were of great value—even after steamboat carriage was instituted. The schooner *Decatur* arrived in Detroit from Chicago with 500 packs of furs on board " said to be worth 100,000 dollars "; the schooner *Tiger* transported 410 packs to Buffalo which were valued at $62,000, and the schooners *Superior* and *Red Jacket* each carried 200 packs, estimated to be worth " from 35 to 900 dollars each." [42] Fish, cider, apples, maple sugar, and ashes were also exported in schooners.[43] As late as 1825 freight and passenger traffic on the upper Lakes was almost wholly by schooner, for Detroit continued to be the western terminus for steamboat navigation.[44]

Schooner freight rates declined as shipping facilities increased. Usually, the master contracted with the shipper or his agent to forward merchandise at definite rates.[45] Light, bulky pieces of freight were measured, the length added to girth, and charged for per foot. In some cases this type of freight was reduced to barrel bulk (about 4.2 cubic feet) and shipped at the same rate as that charged for barrels. Heavy goods, such as metals, were rated per hundred pounds. In 1815 Williams paid forty cents per foot for the transport of bulky goods from Buffalo, one dollar per hundred pounds for iron, and three dollars for each barrel.[46] In 1816 he shipped furs to Buffalo at fifty cents per pack.[47] Increased competition, however, served to reduce these charges before long. Angus Mackintosh advertised in the *Gazette* in 1817 that he would transport goods between Sandwich and Fort Erie

in the schooner *Duke of Wellington* at reduced rates; he offered
to ship "goods usually measured" at 1s. 3d. per foot, barrels at
9s. 4½d. each, and metals at 2s. 6d. per hundredweight. He
would transport at still lower rates if any other vessel met his
charges.[48]

When merchandise was received for shipment it was marked
with the owner's initials, and each piece was numbered consecu-
tively.[49] The master, upon receiving freight "in good order" on
board his ship, merely contracted "to deliver in similar order . . .
danger [of the] Lakes only excepted . . . as soon as may be." [50]
Thus property was forwarded at the risk of the owner, the master
not being responsible unless it was "damaged or lost by the
negligence of those . . . concerned in the forwarding." [51]

Steamboat navigation on the Great Lakes was slow to arrive,
for until 1818 and after there was not sufficient demand for freight
and passenger service in the thinly populated lake region to
warrant the expense of its construction.[52] Late in 1817 the *Gazette*
learned of the proposal to build a steamboat at Black Rock
(Buffalo), New York, the next year, and predicted that the
venture would be profitable.[53] Williams wrote to one of the
promoters: "I think you will be well repaid for your trouble in
visiting our country and the extensive water communications which
almost surround it. The public lands being about to be sold will
open a new era in the improvement and character of this
country." [54] While visiting Detroit in the summer of 1818 Elkanah
Watson foresaw the economy of time and cost in transportation
that would come with steamboats, and predicted that "soon the
decks of the steamers will be thronged by passengers of a new
character, attracted by curiosity and purposes of business to this
remote region, who will scatter their funds with a lavish hand." [55]

The progress in the construction of the steamboat at Black
Rock was duly noted in the columns of the *Gazette*. Her arrival
was keenly anticipated; a street was named in her honor, and
gala preparations were made to greet "the finest steam-boat in

America, and in the world, excepting that recently launched at New-York and destined to cross the Atlantic." [56] On August 27, 1818 the *Walk-in-the-Water* dropped anchor in Detroit harbor, forty-four hours and ten minutes running time out of Black Rock, " the wind ahead during nearly the whole passage." [57] She was of 330 tons burden, 135 feet in length, with 32 foot beam, and drew 8½ feet. Her two masts were rigged with sails to take advantage of favorable wind; her low pressure square engine propelled her at an average speed of seven and a half miles per hour. She made periodic stops at several ports to take on wood for fuel, a trip from Buffalo requiring thirty-six to forty cords.[58]

The cost of cabin passage from Buffalo to Detroit was eighteen dollars, although a person could travel in steerage for seven. The fares included accommodations and meals. The owners advertised: " A cabin is fitted up expressly for the accommodation of families, who with their baggage will be carried on very low terms." [59] In 1820 the rates were reduced somewhat, the cost of a cabin passage to Detroit being lowered to fifteen dollars.[60] During the short season of her first year the receipts had exceeded $10,000. When the *Walk-in-the-Water* left Detroit on her last trip of the year on November 14, 1818, the *Gazette* claimed that all fears regarding her ability to navigate Lake Erie were groundless, for she had " encountered as severe gales as she probably will meet," and had navigated " in a manner to satisfy the most timid." [61]

The *Walk-in-the-Water* sailed for four seasons between Black Rock and Detroit before being wrecked near Buffalo on November 1, 1821.[62] She was the only steamboat on Lake Erie during this time, and did much to promote the settlement and development of Detroit and Michigan Territory. Her owners advertised that she was " supplied with the best of provisions and stores," and that on board her were " combined expedition, ease, comfort, and convenience in traveling, which the traveler very rarely finds united." [63] Schoolcraft, who made a trip on the vessel in 1820, claimed: " The accommodations of the boat are all that could be wished." [64] In 1819 a schedule of sailing dates from Detroit appeared in the *Gazette*, and in 1820 a planned schedule from May through November appeared in the paper.[65] Stops were made at Erie, Grand River (Fairport), Cleveland, and Sandusky Bay when the weather permitted.[66] The effectiveness with which the vessel maintained its schedule in 1818 led the *Gazette* to proclaim that during its period of navigation Detroit was "brought within seven days journey of the city of New York." [67] When it was learned in 1819 that the *Walk-in-the-Water* would make a summer journey to Mackinac, a New York editor wrote: "The trip has so near a resemblance to the famous Argonautic expedition in the heroic ages of Greece that expectation is quite alive on the subject." [68] She made another journey to Mackinac and Green Bay in 1821, with "upwards of two hundred passengers and a full cargo of merchandise for the ports on the upper Lakes," but except for these two trips, Detroit remained her western terminus.[69]

Gloom prevailed in Detroit when the news arrived of the wreck of the *Walk-in-the-Water*. One citizen wrote to Schoolcraft that he considered the accident

> one of the greatest misfortunes which have ever befallen Michigan, for in addition to its having deprived us of all certain and speedy communication with the civilized world, I am fearful it will greatly check the progress of emigration and improvement. They speak of *three* new boats on Lake Erie next season; I hope they may be erected, but such reports are always exaggerated.[70]

The report was exaggerated—but in number only, for in January, 1822 forty ship carpenters at Buffalo were at work on a new steamboat, which would sail for Detroit the following May.[71] The engine of the *Walk-in-the-Water* was salvaged and placed in the new hull. Although more strongly built than her predecessor, and of improved design, she was not quite as long nor as wide but of slightly greater tonnage.[72] The *Superior*, as the new ship was named, arrived at Detroit for the first time on May 25, 1822 " with a full freight of merchandise, and ninety-four passengers." [73] Her schedule called for her to leave Buffalo for Detroit every Tuesday at 9:00 A. M., and Detroit for Buffalo every Friday at 4:00 P. M., with stops at the intermediary ports to land and receive passengers " unless prevented by the stress of weather." [74] Her first season was cut short by the violence of a September gale, which damaged her machinery; but for years, thereafter, except for an occasional trip to the upper Lakes, she continued in service between Buffalo and Detroit.[75]

No more steamboats appeared on Lake Erie until 1825. Since 1820 the lands bordering those waters were gradually filling up with settlers; and the scheduled opening of the Erie Canal was expected to give great impetus to this westward migration and to create a great demand for steamboat transportation. " Among the signs of the times," said the editor of the *Gazette*, " the increase of the number of steamboats on our waters is one of the most prominent indications of the growing importance and prosperity of this section of the country." [76] Two steamboats went into operation on Lake Erie in 1825. The *Pioneer*, of 124 tons and 33 horsepower, arrived in Detroit from Buffalo on August 20. She was intended solely for passenger service, leaving Buffalo each Saturday and Detroit each Tuesday. The *Chippewa*, about 50 tons burden and 30 horsepower, began packet service between Detroit and Sandusky.[77] Two more vessels were on the stocks in that year; the *Henry Clay*, of 301 tons, was under construction at Black Rock, and the *Enterprise*, about 220 tons, at Cleveland; but they did not go into operation until the next year.[78] Thomas L. McKenney, on his way north to assist Cass in concluding a treaty with the Indians, arrived in Detroit on the *Henry Clay* in the spring of 1826. Noting the magnitude of the western migration and the facility of steamboat navigation, he wrote from Detroit:

The steamboats *Superior* and *Henry Clay* are surpassed by few, if any, either in size, or beauty of model, or in the style in which they are built and furnished. But there is business for more; and three or four, it is believed, are now in a state of forwardness, to run also between Buffalo and Detroit. I should infer from what I have seen that they all may do a profitable business.[79]

The steamboats performed valiant service in transporting new-comers and their belongings to Detroit and Michigan Territory. In addition, they enabled hundreds of visitors to make convenient journeys to the territory, and these aided in breaking down prejudices in the East by returning with accounts of the new country based upon personal observations. Only 29 passengers arrived in Detroit when the *Walk-in-the-Water* docked for the first time in 1818.[80] Before long, however, the passenger lists lengthened. More than 200 were on board her when she made her journey to Mackinac and Green Bay in 1821.[81] The *Superior* landed 94 when she arrived in Detroit on her maiden voyage in 1822; a month later her trip sheet listed 99.[82] On her first voyage in 1824 she carried 200 passengers, among whom were 30 families intending to settle in Michigan.[83] Of the thousands arriving in the territory in 1825, a large percentage came by steamboat. On her first trip of that year the *Superior* landed 250 passengers; between 300 and 400 arrived on each of her next three trips.[84] On one trip in September the *Pioneer* brought 80 passengers to the city, while the *Superior* landed 170.[85]

Despite the expediency of shipment the cost of freight by steam-boat diminished until it was at a par with costs by sailing vessel. Except for heavy goods, which were freighted per hundredweight, the barrel was evidently the unit for determining costs; and, as was customary with the schooners, bulky goods were reduced to barrel bulk and rated in a like manner. In 1819 Woodbridge paid $1.50 each for the transportation of merchandise in barrels from Erie to Detroit.[86] Rates were reduced in June, 1820, and were further reduced by competition with sailing vessels in the following years. By the summer of 1825 the *Superior* was carrying merchandise to Detroit at rates as low as those of the schooners. Williams received several hundred barrels of salt by schooner and steamboat, all transported for 37½ cents per barrel from Buffalo.[87] This was a decided relief to the citizens of Detroit, for ten years before, they had paid as much as $3.00 per barrel for the shipment of merchandise by schooner from the same port.

The safeguarding of navigation on the Lakes did not keep pace with the improvements in ship design or with the increase in shipping tonnage. Sailing vessels, especially, were at the mercy of Lake Erie gales. Captains depended upon the strength of their anchor cables in rough weather to keep their ships from being dashed upon shore or driven into shoal water. Often, if the cables parted, the ships would be forced " to bear up and run back hundreds of miles " to the Niagara River, which was the only accessible harbor at the eastern end of Lake Erie and " the only safe retreat or shelter from wild storms." At the western end of the Lake the harbor of Put-in-Bay was the only safe natural anchorage, and in times of rough weather mariners endeavored to reach its protected waters.[88] Many ships were lost for want of refuge, particularly in the autumn when storms were most severe.[89] Even though the *Walk-in-the-Water* foundered in an autumn gale, she had demonstrated the superiority of the steamboat in navigating Lake Erie. Williams wrote to his shipping agent at Buffalo in the fall of 1823:

> Should any goods directed to me have reached your place, I will thank you to ship them on board the steam boat. . . . At this season of the year particularly, I prefer to have my goods shipped on board the boat, on account of the prevalence of south west and westerly winds, which frequently renders the passage of vessels depending on sails alone extremely precarious and tedious, and even hazardous.[90]

The mouths of all the rivers and creeks entering Lake Erie were choked with vegetable debris and fronted with sand bars. Most of the ports on the lake were located at the mouths of streams, because of the facilities they offered for inland communication. The prevalence of the sand bars, however, prohibited the larger vessels from using them as anchorages. William Darby claimed in 1818 that, with the exception of Niagara River, Put-in-Bay, and the Detroit River, there existed no harbor in Lake Erie that could be safely entered in a swelling sea by a vessel drawing seven feet of water.[91] Ships were forced to come to anchor in open water of safe depth, and load and unload their cargoes with lighters and flat boats. Even a light sea rendered this task difficult, and often a vessel would be obliged " to heave up her anchors and stand out to sea to avoid being dashed to pieces on a lee shore." [92] Elkanah Watson foresaw the need of federal assistance in the construction of harbors. As early as 1818, on noting the growing population of Ohio and Michigan, he predicted that steamboat navigation and the Erie Canal would so enhance their development that the federal government would be forced to remove obstacles to lake shipping.[93]

The first attempts at harbor development were private ventures. The citizens of Cleveland failed in an endeavor to raise money by a lottery to improve their harbor, and a pier built there in 1816 by a private company was washed away in a storm.[94] The first experiment in actual harbor improvement was undertaken by private capital at the mouth of the Grand River in Ohio in July, 1818, and an experienced harbor engineer was hired to direct the work. Two tiers of piles were projected from each bank of the river, extending into the lake and over the sand bar. The space within the tiers was filled with timber, brush, and stone. Subsequently, the area between the bar and the shore and the piles was filled with sand by surf action; but the river water, coursing with undiffused energy through the artificial channel made by the piles, cut away the bar.[95] When it became known that the Grand River harbor had been improved by piling, private interests began similar work at other points along the coast. Before 1823 harbor improvement of like nature had been started at the mouths of the Cataraugus, Conneaut, and Ashtabula creeks, at the Cuyahoga, Black, Vermilion, and Huron rivers, at Port Clinton, and at the River Raisin.[96] Much of the merchandise destined for the West was shipped overland to Buffalo, but the harbor there in its natural state was totally inadequate. Vessels were forced to " come to in three fathom," for any closer approach to the shore necessitated anchoring in " bad holding-ground, rendering vessels liable to drag on shore before getting under way." [97] Citizens of the community, anxious to improve its position as a forwarding center, initiated harbor development in 1820. By 1821 they had excavated an eight foot channel, and built two piers extending more than a thousand feet into the bay.[98] But private expenditures, even though augmented by small state appropriations, were not sufficient to develop the harbors properly or to keep them in a satisfactory state of repair.

The first federal appropriations for safeguarding navigation on Lake Erie were made in 1816, and were solely for the erection of lights " at or near Bird Island " in the Niagara River, and " on or near Presque Isle." [99] In 1818 Congress granted $15,500 for the construction of lighthouses at Buffalo and Presque Isle, and in the ensuing years set aside various amounts for similar projects at danger points along the coast.[100]

Not until 1823, however, did the federal government make appropriations for harbor improvement. In that year the insignificant sum of $150 was allotted for a survey of the harbor of Presque Isle. By the terms of the appropriation an engineer was required to " make a probable estimate of the expense of removing the obstructions, and report on the best manner of removing them, and the effect of such removal on the channel in the future." [101] This was followed the next year by a grant of $20,000 for the actual opening of the harbor.[102] In 1825 Congress appropriated $5,000 for the construction of a pier at Cleveland, and $1,000 for the completion of the pier at the mouth of the Grand River, which had been started by private interests.[103] Finally, in the spring of 1826 the first general harbor improvement bill became law, and funds were designated for the development of harbors at Buffalo, Ashtabula, Grand River, Huron River, Cunningham Creek, and for the survey of Sandusky and La Plaisance bays.[104] When these projects were completed, the dangers and expense involved in navigating Lake Erie were greatly reduced.

The major obstacle to intercourse between Detroit and other sections of the country was the inconvenience and expense of transportation by land. Even though the costs of carriage by water diminished, the lack of facilities for overland transportation kept freight rates between Detroit and other points at a high level. In 1815 no road existed between Detroit and Ohio, the source of most of the food for the garrison and the civilian population. Yet when navigation was closed the populace was forced to depend upon this expensive, dangerous, and unpredictable wilderness route for all communication with the outside world.

The first attempt to improve the situation was made in 1816 when troops at Detroit began the construction of a road to the rapids of the Miami River.[105] By the summer of 1818 the road had been " cut through a perfect wilderness of a large growth of timber " to within " a few miles " of the River Raisin,[106] and at the end of the year it reached to within eight miles of the rapids. The road was described as " truly a magnificent one, being eighty feet wide, cleared of all the logs and underbrush, every low place causewayed, and all creeks and rivers requiring it, bridged in a substantial manner." [107] Because of sickness among the troops employed, the project was delayed somewhat; but, finally, in the late fall of 1819 the *Gazette* announced: " The road is now cut through, and bridges made over runs and marshes from this place to the Miami Rapids, a distance of 75 miles." [108]

Evidently, the road was poorly located, for by 1822 citizens of Detroit were demanding a new road between the city and the Ohio line. The existing road was described as " almost impassable for wagons, even in good weather, on account of logs, stumps, and deep holes, and in the fall and spring it was " almost impossible to travel it on horseback." [109] Congress was dilatory in taking action, but in the spring of 1824 it appropriated $20,000 for the construction of a new road from Detroit to Miami Rapids, and authorized the President to employ federal troops in making it.[110] The survey of the new route was completed by November, 1824, and contracts for its construction were let the following spring.[111] Governor Cass, who was appointed to superintend the project, decided to issue contracts for only twenty-one and three-quarters miles of the sixty mile route, for the appropriation was insufficient to make a permanent road the whole distance. The swampland bordering the River Raisin was the most formidable area to be spanned, and most of the grant was used for that purpose. By the close of 1825 Cass claimed that some of the contracts were completed, and that almost all were in a process of execution. He estimated that a further appropriation of $15,000 would be needed to complete the road; and in emphasizing the necessity of continuing it, he said:

> I need not advert to the importance of this road, nor to the little probability that it will ever be formed without the interposition of the general government. It is the connecting link between the territory of Michigan and the more settled portion of the Union. It is essential to the prosperity of the country in peace, and to its security in war.[112]

In December, 1825, he left Detroit for Washington with petitions for aid in making roads.[113] A month later he sent a memorial to Congress, describing the situation of the territory and stressing the need of completing the road to the Miami Rapids, and providing for additional ones.[114] No further appropriations were forthcoming, however, until the spring of 1827, when Congress set aside $12,000 for completing the project.[115]

The establishment of an all-weather road to the rapids of the Miami was not sufficient to end the isolation of Detroit and Michigan Territory. This objective could not be attained until a road was constructed across the Black Swamp to the settled parts of Ohio. According to the terms of the Treaty of Brownstown in 1808, the United States was obligated to build a road across this expanse.[116] In December, 1811, Congress appropriated $6,000 for the survey of the road, but war with England intervened, and all plans for its immediate construction were disrupted. During the war American troops built a military road across the swamp, but it was hastily constructed and of temporary utility.[117] Cass claimed that flour transported along this route to the troops at Detroit cost a hundred dollars per barrel, and that " teams frequently consumed upon the road, the whole forage they were employed to transport." Disease brought on by exposure and " the almost impassable nature of the roads" took a high toll among those who journeyed along the route.[118]

By virtue of the Treaty of the Rapids of the Miami in 1817 the Indian title to lands in northwestern Ohio was extinguished, and Michigan Territory became a contiguous part of the United States.[119] In the meantime, while Congress had authorized the President to alter the course of the road across the Black Swamp, it had appropriated no funds for its construction.[120] Evidently, Congress believed that the troops at Detroit could build it after they had completed the one from Detroit to the Miami Rapids.[121] In November, 1817, however, Woodbridge reported to Congress that it seemed " quite impossible, by the aid only of the small and diminished military force of the government at Detroit, to effect at any time so desirable a work." [122] Cass and McArthur pointed out the military necessity of constructing the road, but for several years Congress took no action.[123]

Finally, in February, 1823, a law was passed which granted to the state of Ohio a tract of land 120 feet wide, extending from the western boundary of the Connecticut Reserve to the rapids of the Miami, whereon to build a road. An additional grant of continuous strips of land a mile wide on either side of the proposed road was tendered to the state to defray the cost of its construction. Ohio accepted the grant and appropriated a sum of money for its survey. Contracts were let by September, 1824, but the project was not completed until 1827.[124]

The citizens of Detroit were pleased with the prospect of an all-land route to the interior of Ohio. One contributor to the *Gazette* declared, " By it, our communication with the rest of the Union is assured, and we shall cease to be an isolated point." [125] The editor of the paper rejoiced that when the Black Swamp road was completed, " travelers may have their choice of a land or water route to the Atlantic cities." [126] But Cass believed that more should be done to insure the safety of Michigan Territory and to promote its development. He recommended to Congress that the road through the Black Swamp be extended until it reached the tributaries of the Ohio River. He felt that it would be sound policy to continue it until it intersected "the great western road from Washington; and that a direct communication should thus be opened between the center and the weakest and most exposed frontier of the Union." [127]

In 1818 there was small need for roads leading from Detroit to the interior of the territory; the few inhabitants of the area lived along the shores of the navigable waterways, and journeys overland were rare. The surrounding wilderness reached to within two miles of the city, but what it was like and what it contained remained a mystery. Not until an expedition explored the area in the fall of 1818 did the people in Detroit begin to take an interest in its possibilities.[128] Except for the few furs that might be gathered there, it contributed nothing to the well-being of the city, and Detroit could justly be termed " a town with (comparatively) no country." The more enlightened citizens, realizing that " a town cannot flourish extensively without a country to support it," petitioned the Administration to put on the market

the lands in southeastern Michigan that had already been surveyed.[129] When this was done in the summer of 1818, the hinterland received its first settlers, and with the advent of new towns
came demands to link them to Detroit by establishing adequate
communication.[130]

The Territorial Legislature had earlier endeavored to establish
inland roads. In 1816 it had asked for bids to cut and open a
turnpike from the boundary of the city of Detroit to a point five
miles north.[131] By 1818 two and a half miles of this road had
been constructed, extending as far as the southern limits of the
Ten Thousand Acre Tract donated to the city by Congress, and
had been laid out through the tract.[132] To hasten the completion
of the project volunteer soldier labor was employed, the citizens of
Detroit agreeing to pay for it.[133] Subsequently, the Legislature
arranged to have the road laid out to Pontiac, and contracted
for the construction of a turnpike across the most difficult part
of the route.[134] Private citizens contributed funds and subscribed
labor for building the road; for having speculated in lands, they
realized that their profits depended to a large extent on the
accessibility of their purchases.[135] Shelters were erected along this
stretch for the housing of subscribed labor, and large groups of
farmers met there in organized bees to build causeways across
the marshes.[137] The road was totally inadequate for transportation
purposes, however, for the territory lacked the funds necessary
to conquer the intervening marshlands. Many of the settlers in
the hinterland preferred to forward their supplies by small boats
to Mt. Clemens via the Clinton River, and thence to Pontiac by
packhorse.[138]

In 1822 the Legislature authorized the laying out of a road
between Pontiac and Saginaw, and by January, 1823, the survey was
completed.[139] Territorial funds, however, were not sufficient to
carry out the project. The action of Congress in granting lands
to Ohio to defray the cost of constructing the road across the
Black Swamp induced the people of Michigan to petition for

similar grants to open roads to the interior, or for outright appropriations for their construction. The *Gazette* expressed the senti-
ment of the populace in an editorial:

> There is little doubt but improvements in laying out and
> making roads in this territory would yield a greater profit
> to the national treasury than a like quantity and kind of
> improvement made in any of the other U. S. territories; why,
> then, should not Michigan receive *more* aid, in this respect,
> than any other section of the national domain? Why should
> there be any hesitation in making appropriations for roads
> through the public lands, when it is known that a trifling
> expenditure, for the purpose, will insure a rapid sale of the
> lands and greatly increase the receipts of the national
> treasury? [140]

Father Gabriel Richard, the territorial delegate in Congress,
worked ceaselessly to obtain federal aid for constructing roads
in order to provide pathways to the public lands that had been
offered for sale.[141] He introduced legislation for the survey of
a road from Detroit to Chicago, pointing out that the project
was necessary from a military standpoint, and that it would greatly
increase the revenue derived from the sale of public lands along
the route.[142] On March 3, 1825 Congress passed a law appropriating $3,000 for the survey and laying out of the road.[143] The
survey was completed during July of that year, but actual construction awaited a further appropriation.[144]

By 1825 the lack of roads to the interior settlements was the
most pressing problem facing Detroit and the settled areas of
Michigan Territory. The *Herald* maintained that despite the importance of the road through the Black Swamp, there was a more
immediate need for roads leading to the populated places in the
hinterland. It declared that the people of Michigan could not
be expected to finance the building of these roads, for many of
them had expended most of their money in removing to new
homes and in purchasing lands. It claimed that some of the

money used in building national roads in other parts of the nation was obtained from the sale of public lands, and that expediency and justice demanded "that roads which facilitate the sales of public lands, and promote the essential interests of those who purchase, should be undertaken at the cost of the general government," which had previously "not been inattentive to similar claims of the new settlers." According to the *Herald* the main roads leading from Detroit must be the Ohio, Chicago, Shiawassee, Mackinac, and Fort Gratiot; and the sooner they were laid out the better, in order "that the location of towns and the direction of minor roads" might be regulated by them. It further asserted that the growth of Detroit would be "accelerated or retarded in proportion as the making of the roads . . . mentioned is hastened or delayed." [145]

When Cass left for Washington in December, 1825, he carried with him a number of petitions for federal aid to construct inland roads.[146] In a memorial to the House of Representatives, pursuant to a resolution regarding measures necessary to safeguard the northwestern territories, Cass contended that the establishment of adequate roads from Detroit to strategic points on the shores of Lake Huron, Lake Michigan, and Lake Erie was sufficient to secure the region from attack. He pointed out that by means of land grants these roads could be built at no expense to the nation.[147] The Committee on Military Affairs concurred with his views on the subject and recommended to Congress that roads be surveyed from Detroit to Saginaw Bay and to Fort Gratiot. In addition to a request that money be appropriated to complete the road from Detroit to Ohio, it asked that a "reasonable" sum be set aside for the opening and construction of the road to Chicago.[148] Early in 1827 Congress granted $20,00 for the construction of the road to Chicago, but several years elapsed before it authorized the building of roads to Saginaw and Fort Gratiot.[149]

The Corporation of the City of Detroit tried to keep the streets of the city in a passable condition, levying a tax to be paid in labor for accomplishing the work. By an act of the Legislature the city was responsible for the repair of six and a half miles of the turnpike leading to Pontiac, even though three and a half miles of it was beyond the city limits.[150] Few of the roads in the immediate vicinity of the city, however, were kept in good repair. The *Gazette* censured the citizenry for their laxity in this regard, and urged them to increase their efforts to better communication with the interior. " It is truly discouraging to the emigrant," said the editor, "after having transported his goods for three or four hundred miles, to have them dashed to pieces on our broken causeways, within ten miles of this place." [151]

Wagons could negotiate the roads fairly well in dry periods, but only with great difficulty at other times. In the winter sleighs provided a fine means of communication while the snow and cold lasted.[152] Despite the poor condition of the road to Pontiac, stage coaches began to run over it as early as 1822, and continued on to Mt. Clemens.[153] In the early part of 1826 additional stages began making runs from Detroit to Ann Arbor, Lower Sandusky, and via the "horse-boat ferry," to Amherstburg.[154]

As the interior of Michigan was settled, post offices and post roads were established. By an act of Congress, May 13, 1820, a post road was laid out from Detroit to Pontiac to Mt. Clemens, and in 1823 it was extended to Saginaw.[155]

The lack of adequate transportation facilities between the Atlantic seaboard and the Great Lakes served to complicate the problem of supply in Detroit. The high prices paid for imported merchandise in Detroit resulted largely from the high cost of carriage across the state of New York. Conversely, only products of a luxury nature which could absorb the high cost of transport could be sent from Detroit to eastern markets.[156] The Hudson River provided an expeditious avenue for the transport of goods from New York City to Albany, and competition between sloops and steamboats plying the river kept freight charges at a reasonable level.[157] Navigation on the river was open only nine months of the year, but stage coaches and wagons made regular trips to Albany and return during the remaining months.[158]

Albany was the *entrepot* for the western country. Agents engaged in the storage and transport business made their headquarters there. They received goods from New York for shipment westward and forwarded the products of the West to their eastern destination. This business increased greatly after the War of 1812. Prior to that conflict most of the merchandise for the western country had been boated up the Mississippi from New Orleans, or carried by wagon over the mountains from Philadelphia to Pittsburgh, and then boated down the Ohio River.[159] Detroit merchants, however, having little access to either of these routes, had for many years utilized the land-water route across the state of New York. Merchandise arriving in Albany from New York City was wagoned to Schenectady. From there it was transported in durham boats or bateaux up the Mohawk River, through the Utica and Rome Canal, down Wood Creek, across Oneida Lake, down the Oneida, Seneca, and Oswego rivers, and around the portage at Oswego Falls to Lake Ontario. Thence it was carried by schooner to Lewiston, wagoned around Niagara Falls, and shipped by durham boats or bateaux to Black Rock.[160] Although land transport was required for less than twenty-five miles of this route, freight charges were high in comparison with water carriage elsewhere. This was due to the scarcity and small capacity of the river boats, the canal tolls, and the repeated transfer of cargo.[161]

During the War of 1812 this route was closed to traffic because of the military and naval operations taking place in the Ontario region. To meet this emergency wagons ordinarily employed in transporting goods from Albany to Schenectady gradually extended their routes westward. Before long, teams and wagons were carrying merchandise over the Ontario and Genesee turnpike to Buffalo.[162] Freight charges in 1813 over this route were as high as $6.00 per hundredweight.[163]

The end of the war found the facilities for the storage and trans-shipment of freight along the water route much impaired. To meet the great demand for merchandise in the lake region, Detroit merchants were forced to continue bringing their goods by the expensive land route. Huge covered wagons, constructed especially for freighting purposes, made their appearance on the route. Soon their owners practically monopolized the transport business between Albany and Buffalo. These wagons were drawn by several teams of horses, but were so ponderous that they traveled " at a snail's pace " and frequently impeded the progress of swifter moving traffic. Ordinarily, they required from twelve to eighteen days to make the journey, and it was not uncommon for a stage coach to encounter twenty to thirty of them on the road in a single day. " Oh, for the completion of the canal," wrote Elkanah Watson, " when terrible Pennsylvania wagons will disappear." [164]

In 1815 the cost of wagon transport from Albany to Buffalo was $5.00 per hundredweight. From Albany to Seneca Falls by water and thence to Buffalo by wagon was $4.50.[165] Stage coaches made the journey in from eight to ten days, depending upon the condition of the roads and the volume of traffic.[166] Improvements in organization and an increase in the quantity of freight shipped westward served to reduce transportation rates. In 1818 Charles Smyth of Albany advertised that he had completed arrangements to transport freight from New York City to Detroit at $4.50 per hundredweight.[167] Welcome as was this reduction, the expense of land transport across New York State continued to add many dollars to the cost of merchandise in Detroit, and reduced greatly the profits from the sale of western products. After a journey through New York and the western country in 1816, David Thomas wrote: " If sloops of fifty tons burden could pass direct from New York to Lake Erie, the whole complexion of the western world would be changed." [168]

For many years enterprising individuals in New York had

pointed out the advisability of connecting the waters of Lake
Erie with those of the Hudson River by means of a canal. After
much argument and delay the New York State Legislature finally
authorized the project on April 15, 1817, and provided means
for financing it.[169] By the end of June that year the route of the
Erie Canal had been laid out and contracts let for the construction
of the middle section. The first excavation was made at Rome,
New York on July 4, 1817.[170]

The benefits that would be derived from the project were
universally recognized. By way of the canal a channel would be
opened for the produce of hitherto unimproved areas in the
western part of New York State and of the lake country. Much
of the trade of the West that had been carried on with New
Orleans or Montreal would be diverted to New York City. In
addition to economical transportation, the western country would
have access to more stable markets and would be able to purchase
imported merchandise at lower cost.[171] In Detroit there was some
apprehension regarding the completion of the great project, but
few were insensible to the momentous changes it would effect.
When Williams learned that the canal had been authorized, he
wrote to a friend:

> The projected canal to connect the waters of Lake Erie
> with those of the Hudson will no doubt greatly accelerate
> the population and prosperity of this country, an event and
> undertaking no doubt exceedingly gigantic, but which will
> inevitably produce as majestic a change in our country as
> the object appears difficult to accomplish.[172]

Shortly after work began on the canal, the *Gazette* remarked:

> In the event of the accomplishment of this work, the state
> of New York will undoubtedly be the greatest gainer; but the
> western part of Pennsylvania, Ohio, and Michigan must also
> participate largely in its benefits. Many important branches
> of trade, which are now entirely unimproved, will then
> become sources of wealth and prosperity to the western
> country.[173]

In October, 1819, the canal was opened to navigation from Utica to Rome, and by the spring of 1820 the ninety-four miles constituting the middle section, from Utica to the Seneca River, was open to traffic. From this time on there was no doubt as to the ultimate completion of the project, for all opposition to it was dissipated by the utility of transportation over this section.[174] When it was realized in Detroit that the canal would surely be completed, enthusiasm became very pronounced. The *Gazette*, endeavoring to promote the prosperity of Detroit by advertising its prospects, predicted: " the *Clinton Canal* and the *Power of Steam* ... will bring Detroit as near to New York, for the purposes of commercial intercourse, as Albany was twenty years ago." [175] The editor pointed out, however, that several years must elapse before the territory would be sufficiently productive to meet its own demands for foodstuffs, and that the greatest benefit that the canal would confer upon Detroit would be in providing an unobstructed and inexpensive avenue for those inhabitants of New England and New York who wished to remove to Michigan.[176] Williams expressed his belief that the canal would greatly increase the value of real estate in Michigan.[177] Those engaged in the fishing industry anticipated a great reduction in the price of salt, practically all of which was imported from central New York at great expense.[178]

As additional sections of the canal were opened to navigation, transportation charges across New York State decreased proportionately. By the end of 1821 freight was shipped from Albany to Buffalo for about $2.50 per hundredweight, and in 1822 it was reduced to $2.00.[179] At the opening of navigation in 1823 canal boats could travel 220 miles without interruption, and by June of that year they could pass from Rochester to Schenectady.[180] In the spring of 1825 packet boat and stage coach services were combined to offer transportation from Schenectady to Buffalo in four days.[181]

The fall of 1825 witnessed the completion of the Erie Canal. Two thousand boats of forty tons burden plied its waters, drawn by eight thousand horses and operated by eight thousand men.[182] Including all tolls, merchandise was transported by canal boat from Albany to Buffalo, a distance of 362 miles, for about ninety cents per hundredweight, about one-fifth the cost of wagon transport in 1816. Farm produce was shipped at even lower rates, a hundredweight being carried across the state for about fifty-five cents. Passengers were carried on the freight boats at a rate of one to one and a half cents per mile.[183]

Commenting on the utility of the Canal, the *Niles' Weekly Register* declared: " Distance is conquered by science, and in the neighborhood of the Lakes, is no longer a thing to be regarded. Detroit is virtually nearer to New York, than Cumberland, in Maryland, is to Baltimore." [184] When a shipment of oysters arrived by steamboat from Buffalo, after having been transported through the Canal, the *Michigan Herald* regarded it as a " confirmation of the reality of the great event which has united this distant region with the Atlantic." The editor proclaimed: *" Detroit is now removed but six days journey from New York."* [185]

Even with the improvements in the facilities for transportation and communication, postal service between Detroit and other parts of the country remained a vexing problem. In 1817 Cass wrote to the Postmaster General complaining of the delays experienced in the delivery of mail, and was promised that the situation would be remedied.[186] Detroit continued to receive but one delivery weekly.[187] As the region grew in commercial importance, the mounting irregularities in the arrival of the mail presented an acute problem. The lone carrier was obliged to traverse the Black Swamp and the wilderness leading to Detroit on horseback, but so great was the volume of mail that he was unable to bring it all at one time. Early in 1823 the *Gazette* expressed the belief that private correspondence was held up along the route to facilitate the delivery of official mail, and to " average the loads for the carrier's pony." It knew not how otherwise to account for the fact that the Washington newspapers were frequently six weeks on the road when they should have been delivered within eleven days of the time they were printed.[188] Often the editor delayed publication for several days in hopes that the tardy carrier would arrive with the latest news from the East.[189] Early in 1824 the situation had become more aggravating than ever, inducing the editor to berate the contractors responsible for the delivery of mail to Detroit and to declare: " The inconveniences which the people of this place and the adjacent counties suffer cannot longer be borne; a remedy must be sought and found." [190]

Petitions for improving the service went unheeded, however, for the authorities claimed that the postal receipts from the area were not sufficient to justify the expense of two deliveries each week.[191] In Washington, Gabriel Richard, congressional delegate from Michigan, experienced the same irregularity and delay in the receipt of mail from Detroit. Letters were more than three weeks on the road, and newspapers often failed to arrive at all.[192] John McLean succeeded R. J. Meigs as Postmaster General in 1823, and in March, 1824 Richard secured from him a promise for better service.[193] In November, 1824, news arrived in Detroit that, beginning the next month, there would be two mails weekly.[194] Shortly after the new arrangement went into effect the *Gazette* asserted: " None but those who have once been favored by the receipt of information by mail two or three times a week, can judge of the satisfaction which this circumstance has diffused among our citizens." [195]

CHAPTER II—NOTES

[1] Butler to Sibley, October 26, 1815, " Solomon Sibley Papers " (MS, Burton Historical Collection, Detroit Public Library; hereafter cited as B. H. C.).

[2] A. E. Parkins, *The Historical Geography of Detroit* (Lansing, 1918), pp. 174-75.

[3] *Detroit Gazette*, April 19, 1822.

[4] *Niles' Weekly Register*, January 11, 1817.

[5] *American State Papers* . . . (38 vols.; Washington, 1832-1861), *Commerce and*

Navigation, II, 40-41; Macomb to Major General Jacob Brown, July 27, 1816, " Alexander Macomb Letterbook, 1807-1819 " (Typescript, B. H. C.).

[6] Williams to Boyd & Suydam, December 30, 1815, " John R. Williams Letterbook, 1815-1825 " (MS, property of Frederick Douglas, Denver, Colorado).

[7] Witherell to his wife, August 21-23, 1815, " B. F. H. Witherell Papers " (MS, B. H. C.).

[8] [J. B. Mansfield], *History of the Great Lakes* (2 vols.; Chicago, 1899), I, 586. The following table illustrates the growth of vessel tonnage on Lake Erie from 1815 to 1819. The data are from the *American State Papers, Commerce and Navigation*, II, 40-41, 90-91, 164-65, 408-09.

	Tonnage Registered			
Port	1815	1816	1817	1819
Buffalo, N. Y.	None	493.77	493.77	No returns
Erie, Pa.	249.19	644.59	667.28	633.21
Cleveland, Ohio	419.18	590.39	644.40	834.71
Sandusky, Ohio	None	71.42	280.26	363.59
Detroit, Mich.	159.12	498.69	630.23	533.45

[9] Collector's Office, Detroit, to David Thomas, July 8, 1818, quoted in David Thomas, *Travels Through the Western Country in the Summer of 1816* . . . (Auburn, N. Y., 1819), pp. 309-314.

[10] *American State Papers, Commerce and Navigation*, II, 164-65.

[11] Thomas, *op. cit.*, p. 314.

[12] United States Custom House, Detroit, " Impost Book, 1815-1823 " (MS, B. H. C.), pp. 1-34, *passim*.

[13] Thomas, *op. cit.*, p. 314.

[14] See Fred Coyne Hamil, " Early Shipping and Land Transportation on the Lower Thames," *Ontario Historical Society, Papers and Records*, XXXIV (1942), 3-19.

[15] United States Custom House, " Impost Book," pp. 1-34, *passim*.

[16] *Ibid.*, pp. 11, 13.

[17] Henry R. Schoolcraft, *Narrative Journal of Travels . . . from Detroit through the Great Chain of American Lakes to the Sources of the Mississippi River . . . in the Year 1820* (Albany, 1821), pp. 67-70, gives an excellent description and his use of the cargo canoe.

[18] One canoe carried 3,822 pounds of flour from Sandwich to Detroit. United States Custom House, " Impost Book," p. 4.

[19] United States Custom House, Detroit, " Daybook 1815-1828 " (MS, 11 vols.; B. H. C.), I, March 29, 1816.

[20] Parkins, *op. cit.*, p. 206.

[21] Charles C. Trowbridge, " Detroit Past and Present in Relation to its Social and Physical Condition," *Michigan Pioneer and Historical Society, Collections* (40 vols.; Lansing, 1877-1929), I, 383. (Hereafter cited as *M. P. H. S., C.*)

[22] United States Custom House, " Daybook," I, June 20, 1816.

[23] Parkins, *op. cit.*, p. 207.

[24] United States Custom House, " Daybook," I, June 5, 12, 1816; II, October 16, 1816.

[25] Mansfield, *op. cit.*, I, 390-91; William Kingsford, *History of Canada* (10 vols.; Toronto, 1887-1898), VII, 26.

[26] United States Custom House, "Daybook," II, October 17, 1816.

[27] Kingsford, *op. cit.*, VII, 27.

[28] Reuben Gold Thwaites, ed., *Early Western Travels, 1748-1846* (32 vols.; Cleveland, 1904).

[29] Kingsford, *op. cit.*, VII, 26-27.

[30] United States Custom House, "Daybook," I, April 1, 2, 20, 22, 23, May 7, July 6, 1816; II, May 1, 1817.

[31] *Ibid.*, I, September 7, 1816, II, October 3, 1816; *Detroit Gazette*, October 10, 1823.

[32] Much of the flour brought to Detroit from Ohio in 1816 was carried in open boats.—United States Custom House, "Daybook," I, April 20, 22, 23, 1816.

[33] *Detroit Gazette*, October 25, November 1, 1825.

[34] *Ibid.*, November 21, 1817.

[35] Witherell to his wife, August 29, 1815, "Witherell Papers"; Williams to H. H. Schiffelin & Co., December 30, 1815, "Williams Letterbook."

[36] *Detroit Gazette*, November 21, 1817.

[37] *Ibid.*, May 10, 1822.

[38] *Ibid.*, June 7, 1822.

[39] *Ibid.*, May 2, 1823, April 26, May 10, 1825.

[40] For the record of arrivals and cargoes at the Port of Detroit, week of July 17-24, 1817, see the *Detroit Gazette*, July 25, 1817. See also the *Gazette* for January 29 and August 13, 1819, and Thomas, *op. cit.*, pp. 314-16.

[41] *Detroit Gazette*, April 9, 1824.

[42] *Ibid.*, August 10, 17, 1821. The schooner *Mariner* of the American Fur Company was reported to have carried a cargo of furs valued from $267,000 to $270,000.—*Michigan Herald*, July 26, 1825; Mansfield, *op. cit.*, I, 605.

[43] Cleared from Detroit in 1817: 870 barrels of fish, 536 barrels of cider, 230 barrels of apples; in 1818, 1,478 barrels of fish, 753 barrels of cider, and 653 barrels of apples. The *Mariner* brought "nearly thirty tons of Indian sugar" from Green Bay in 1825.—Thomas, *op. cit.*, p. 314; *Detroit Gazette*, January 29, 1819, September 20, 1825.

[44] "Last Saturday morning, fourteen schooners, laden with merchandise and produce, sailed from this port for Michilimackinac and the ports on Lake Michigan." —the *Detroit Gazette*, May 18, 1821. See the *Gazette* also for October 29, 1824, June 14, 28, November 1, 1825.

[45] Williams to Russell Mathes, November 1, 1813, "John R. Williams Papers" (MS, B. H. C.); Williams to Hart & Lay, July 15, 1815, "Williams Letterbook."

[46] Samuel Wing to Williams, June 7, 1815, "Williams Papers."

[47] Invoice, July 31, 1816, "Williams Papers."

[48] *Detroit Gazette*, September 5, 1817. In 1825 the freight charge on a barrel of salt carried from Buffalo to Detroit was thirty-seven and a half cents; bulky goods were shipped at fifty cents per barrel bulk.—Williams to William James, September 23, 1825, "Williams Letterbook"; invoice, October 11, 1825, "Williams Papers."

[49] Joseph Mason to R. Abbott, October 26, 1815, "Sibley Papers"; invoice, July 31, 1816, "Williams Papers"; Williams to Jno. Scott, May 15, July 9, 1817, "Williams Letterbook."

[50] Joseph Mason to R. Abbott, October 26, 1815, "Sibley Papers."

[51] Herman Norton to Williams, January 24, 1816, circular, "Williams Papers"; Williams to Boyd & Suydam, July 26, 1817, "Williams Letterbook."

[52] In 1820 there were only four steamboats on the Great Lakes, and only one on Lake Erie, while there were seventy-one on the western rivers and fifty-two on the Atlantic seaboard.—Mansfield, *op. cit.*, I, 394.

[53] *Detroit Gazette*, November 21, 1817.

[54] Williams to Gilbert & J. B. Stuart, May 16, 1818, "Williams Letterbook."

[55] Elkanah Watson, *Men and Times of the Revolution, or Memoirs of Elkanah Watson, Including Journals of Travels in Europe and America, . . .* Winslow C. Watson, ed. (New York, 1856), p. 431.

[56] *Detroit Gazette*, January 23, March 6, May 8, June 12, 26, August 14, 21, 1818.

[57] *Ibid.*, August 28, 1818.

[58] *Ibid.*, May 19, 1820; James Flint, "Letters from America, 1818 to 1820," in Thwaites, *op. cit.*, IX, 314; Mansfield, *op. cit.*, I, 593; John Harrison Morrison, *History of American Steam Navigation* (New York, 1903), p. 366. On her maiden voyage the *Walk-in-the-Water* stopped at Dunkirk, Erie, Cleveland, and Venice (a small village on Sandusky Bay) before docking in Detroit. A lengthy description of the ship and an account of its first trip appeared in the *Gazette*, August 28, 1818, the day following its arrival in Detroit. Williams had contracted for wood for the steamboat, and had at least 200 cords on hand, delivered at $4.75 per cord.—Williams to Gilbert & J. B. Stuart, May 16, 1818, "Williams Letterbook."

[59] *Niagara Patriot*, September 15, 1818. The rates in effect in 1818 were as follows:

From Buffalo to	Dunkirk,	$ 3.00	cabin;	$1.25	steerage
	Erie	6.00	"	2.50	"
	Fairport	10.00	"	4.00	"
	Cleveland	12.00	"	5.00	"
	Sandusky	15.00	"	5.50	"

See also James Cooke Mills, *Our Inland Seas. Their Shipping & Commerce for Three Centuries* (Chicago, 1910), pp. 97-98.

[60] *Detroit Gazette*, June 30, 1820.

[61] *Ibid.*, November 20, 1818.

[62] *Ibid.*, November 9, 1821; Williams to Boyd & Suydam, November 10, 1821, "Williams Letterbook."

[63] *Detroit Gazette*, May 19, 1820.

[64] Schoolcraft, *op. cit.*, p. 48.

[65] *Detroit Gazette*, August 20, 1819, May 19, 1820.

[66] *Ibid.*, May 19, 1820.

[67] *Ibid.*, November 20, 1818.

[68] *New York Merchant Advertiser*, quoted in *ibid.*, May 14, 1819.

[69] *Detroit Gazette*, August 10, 1821.

[70] Henry R. Schoolcraft, *Personal Memoirs of a Residence of Thirty Years with the Indian Tribes on the American Frontier* (Philadelphia, 1851), p. 73.

[71] *Detroit Gazette*, January 18, 1822.

[72] Mansfield, *op. cit.*, I, 603; Morrison, *op. cit.*, p. 367. "She is 346 tons burthen, 110 feet keel, 29 feet beam, and has an engine of 59 horse power."— *Detroit Gazette*, May 31, 1822.

[73] *Detroit Gazette*, May 31, 1822.

[74] Compared to the uncertainty of other means of travel, the speed of steamboat navigation was remarkable—and worthy of notice.—*Ibid.*, May 31, 1822, October 29, 1824.

[75] *Ibid.*, September 27, 1822, October 24, 1823. The *Superior* was lost in Lake Michigan in 1843.—Mansfield, *op. cit.*, I, 891.

[76] *Detroit Gazette*, January 7, 1825.

[77] *Ibid.*, June 14, August 23, 1825.

[78] *Ibid.*, January 7, June 14, 28, 1825, May 23, 1826; *Michigan Herald*, May 10, 1826.

[79] Thomas L. McKenney, *Sketches of a Tour to the Lakes, of the Character and Customs of the Chippeway Indians, and of Incidents Connected with the Treaty of Fond du Lac* (Baltimore, 1827), pp. 141-42.

[80] *Detroit Gazette*, August 28, 1818.

[81] *Ibid.*, August 10, 1821.

[82] *Ibid.*, May 31, June 21, 1822.

[83] *Ibid.*, May 7, 1824.

[84] *Ibid.*, April 26, May 10, 24, 31, 1825; *Michigan Herald*, May 24, 31, 1825.

[85] *Detroit Gazette*, September 27, 1825.

[86] Invoices, June 24, 1819, June 5, 1820, "Receipts," "William Woodbridge Papers" (MS, B. H. C.).

[87] "The Captain of the Steam Boat *Superior*, has this morning requested the preference of the freight, at the same rate, which is charged by schooners on the lake; I would advise by all means to send it by the steamboat."—Williams to William James, August 6, 1825, "Williams Letterbook." See also Williams to James, September 23, 1825, *ibid.*

[88] Captain Augustus Walker, "Early Days on the Lakes," *Buffalo Historical Society, Publications*, V (1902), 290, 297, 298.

[89] Joseph Mason to G. Godfroyd, November 10, 1815, "Sibley Papers"; Williams to Boyd & Suydam, December 30, 1815, "Williams Letterbook"; *Detroit Gazette*, September 27, 1822, December 5, 1823, October 25, 1825.

[90] Williams to Townsend & Coit, September 17, 1823, "Williams Letterbook."

[91] William Darby, *A Tour from the City of New York, to Detroit in The Michigan Territory, Made Between the 2nd of May and the 22nd of September, 1818* (New York, 1819), p. 207.

[92] Christian Schultz, *Travels on an Inland Voyage through the States of New York, Pennsylvania, Virginia, Ohio, Kentucky, and Tennessee and through the Territories of Indiana, Louisiana, Mississippi and New Orleans, Performed in the Years 1807 and 1808, Including a Tour of Nearly Six Thousand Miles* (2 vols.; New York, 1810), I, 106-07. No vessel could enter the harbor of Cleveland if it drew more than three feet of water.—Walker, *op. cit.*, pp. 291, 297.

[93] Watson, *op. cit.*, p. 427.

[94] Ralph G. Plumb, *History of the Navigation of the Great Lakes* (Washington, 1911), p. 44.

[95] Thomas, *op. cit.*, p. 309; Walker, *op. cit.*, pp. 287-88.

[96] Walker, *op. cit.*, p. 289.

[97] *Ibid.*, p. 291.

[98] Plumb, *op. cit.*, p. 42.

[99] " An Act making appropriations for rebuilding light-houses and for completing the plan for lighting them, according to the improvements of Winslow Lewis, for placing beacons and buoys, for preserving Little Gull Island, and for surveying the coast of the United States," April 27, 1816, United States, *The Statutes at Large of the United States . . . Concurrent Resolutions, Recent Treaties, Conventions and Executive Proclamations* (55 vols.; Boston, 1845-73, Washington 1875-1942), III, 316. (Hereafter cited as *United States Statutes at Large.*)

[100] *American State Papers, Commerce and Navigation*, II, 459. "An Act to authorize the building, erecting, and placing, lighthouses, beacons, and buoys or places designated in Boston, Buzzard and Chesapeake bays, Lakes Ontario and Erie, and for other purposes," March 3, 1819; "An Act to authorize the building of lighthouses, light vessels, and beacons, therein mentioned, and for other purposes," March 3, 1823; "An Act to authorize the building of lighthouses, light vessels, and beacons, therein mentioned, and for other purposes," May 26, 1824; "An Act for authorizing the building of lighthouses and light vessels, erecting beacon lights, placing buoys, removing obstructions in river Savannah, and for other purposes," May 18, 1826, *United States Statutes at Large*, III, 534-35, 780-81; IV, 61, 170-73.

[101] " An Act to authorize the building of lighthouses, light vessels, and beacons therein mentioned, and for other purposes," March 3, 1823, *ibid.*, III, 780-81.

[102] " An Act making appropriations for deepening the channel leading into the harbor of Presque Isle, and for repairing Plymouth Beach," May 26, 1824, *ibid.*, IV, 38.

[103] " An Act to authorize the building of lighthouses and light vessels, and beacons, and monuments, therein mentioned; and for other purposes," March 3, 1825, *ibid.*, IV, 133-34.

[104] " An Act for improving certain harbors, and the navigation of certain rivers and creeks, and for authorizing surveys to be made of certain bays, sounds, and rivers, therein mentioned," May 20, 1826, *ibid.*, 175-76. Strict constructionist in Congress, led by John C. Calhoun, opposed federal grants for internal improvements on the grounds that the Constitution was a " salt water instrument," and that, therefore, the improvement of harbors on interior lakes and rivers was unconstitutional.—Plumb, *op. cit.*, pp. 36-64.

[105] Crawford to Macomb, May 29, 1816, Macomb to Crawford, June 20, 1816, Clarence Edwin Carter, ed. and comp., *The Territorial Papers of the United States* (10 vols.; Washington, 1934-1942), X, 639-40, 852-53; Macomb to Brown, June 21, 1816, " Macomb Letterbook."

[106] Estwick Evans, " Evans' Pedestrious Tour of Four Thousand Miles—1818," in Reuben Gold Thwaites, *op. cit.*, VIII, 209.

[107] Macomb to Brown, December 5, 1818, " Macomb Letterbook "; *Niles' Weekly Register*, May 8, 1819.

[108] *Detroit Gazette*, October 15, December 3, 1819.

[109] *Ibid.*, April 19, 1822.

[110] " An Act to authorize the surveying and making of a road from a point in the north-western boundary of the state of Ohio, near the foot of the rapids of the Miami of Lake Erie, to Detroit, in the territory of Michigan," May 26, 1824, *United States Statutes at Large*, IV, 71.

[111] *Detroit Gazette*, November 12, 1824, April 1, 1825.

[112] Letter from Cass to Macomb, in *ibid.*, January 31, 1826.

[113] *Michigan Herald*, December 13, 1825.

[114] United States House of Representatives, *Military Road in Michigan, House Report. No. 42, 19th Congress, 1st Session*, pp. 6-18.

[115] " An Act to authorize the laying out and opening of certain roads in the territory of Michigan," March 2, 1827, *United States Statutes at Large*, IV, 231-32.

[116] " Articles of a treaty made and concluded at Brownstown, in the territory of Michigan, between William Hull, governor of the said territory, superintendent of Indian affairs, and commissioner plenipotentiary of the United States of America, for concluding any treaty or treaties, which may be found necessary, with any of the Indian tribes, north west of the river Ohio, of the one part, and the sachems, chiefs, and warriors of the Chippewa, Ottawa, Pottawatamie, Wyandot, and Shawanoese [*sic*] nations of Indians, of the other part," November 25, 1808, *United States Statutes at Large*, VII, 112-13.

[117] *American State Papers, Miscellaneous*, II, 593.

[118] *House Rep. No. 42*, pp. 8-9.

[119] " Articles of a treaty made and concluded, at the foot of the rapids of the Miami of Lake Erie, between Lewis Cass and Duncan McArthur, commissioners of the United States, with full power and authority to hold conferences, and conclude and sign a treaty or treaties with all or any of the tribes or nations of Indians within the boundaries of the state of Ohio, of and concerning all matters interesting to the United States and the said nations of Indians, on the one part; and the sachems, chiefs, and warriors, of the Wyandot, Seneca, Delaware, Shawanese [*sic*], Pottawatamies, Ottawas, and Chippewa, tribes of Indians," September 29, 1817, *United States Statutes at Large*, VII, 160-68.

[120] " An Act to authorize the President of the United States to alter the road laid out from the foot of the rapids of the Miami of Lake Erie, to the western line of the Connecticut reserve," April 16, 1816, *United States Statutes at Large*, III, 285.

[121] United States House of Representatives, *Message from the President . . . Information of the Roads Made or in Progress, . . . House Document No. 61, 15th Congress, 1st Session*, p. 7. The *Gazette* predicted in 1817: " In another year we shall have a good road from Detroit to Fort Meigs, and probably half way through the Black Swamp." In 1819, with the completion of the road to the rapids, it observed: " The notorious Black Swamp will be next attacked."—*Detroit Gazette*, December 19, 1817 and December 3, 1819.

[122] *American State Papers, Miscellaneous*, II, 593.

[123] *Ibid.*, II, 596.

[124] " An Act for laying out and making a road, from the lower rapids of the Miami of Lake Erie to the western boundary of the Connecticut western reserve, in the state of Ohio, agreeable to the provisions of the Treaty of Brownstown," February 28, 1823, *United States Statutes at Large*, III, 727-28. See also *Detroit Gazette*, January 9, September 3, 1824; Francis P. Weisenburger, *The Passing of the Frontier, 1825-1850* (Columbus, 1941), p. 6.

[125] *Detroit Gazette*, January 31, 1823.

[126] *Ibid.*, September 3, 1824.

[127] *House Report No. 42*, p. 10.

[128] *Detroit Gazette*, March 13, October 30, 1818.

[129] *Ibid.*, March 13, October 16, 1818.

[180] *Ibid.*, July 10, 1818.

[181] " Public Notice," March 26, 1816, " Williams Papers."

[182] Clarence M. Burton, comp., and M. Agnes Burton, ed., *Governor and Judges Journal, Proceedings of the Land Board of Detroit* ([Detroit], 1915), pp. 114, 118.

[183] Macomb to Colonel Henry Leavenworth, January 9, 1819, " Macomb Letter-book."

[184] *Detroit Gazette*, December 16, 1819.

[185] *Ibid.*, February 26, 1819 and January 18, 1822.

[186] *Ibid.*, November 10, 1820.

[187] *Ibid.*, January 18, 1822; Trowbridge, *op. cit.*, p. 381.

[188] In 1825 a company was formed at Detroit to provide bateau transportation along this route. It was estimated that the cost would be 50 per cent lower than by land carriage.—*Detroit Gazette*, May 24, 1825. See also George N. Fuller, *Economic and Social Beginnings of Michigan, A Study of the Settlement of the Lower Peninsula During the Territorial Period, 1805-1837* (Lansing, 1916), p. 206.

[189] *Detroit Gazette*, August 9, 1822, January 17, 1823.

[140] *Ibid.*, February 21, 1824. See also A. N. Bliss, " Federal Land Grants for Internal Improvements," *M. P. H. S., C.*, VII, 52-53.

[141] *Detroit Gazette*, January 16, March 26, 1824.

[142] *Ibid.*, May 14, 1824, February 25 and March 4, 1825.

[143] " An Act to authorize the surveying and opening of a road, from Detroit to Chicago, in the state of Illinois," *United States Statutes at Large*, IV, 135.

[144] *Detroit Gazette*, July 26, 1825.

[145] *Michigan Herald*, September 20, 1825.

[146] *Ibid.*, December 13, 1825.

[147] *House Report No. 42*, pp. 14-15, 17-18.

[148] *Ibid.*, pp. 1-2.

[149] " An Act to authorize the laying out and opening of certain roads in the territory of Michigan," *United States Statutes at Large*, IV, 231-32. In March, 1829 Congress appropriated $10,000 for building the Saginaw road, $15,000 for the road to Fort Gratiot, and $8,000 for extending the Chicago road as far as the Indiana line.—See " An Act making appropriations for completing certain roads, and for making examinations and surveys," March 2, 1829, *ibid.*, IV, 351.

[150] " Considerable labor will also be expended, during this season on the streets and the turnpikes, leading to the county of Oakland. To realize these benefits it was necessary to impose a tax. The corporation in fixing the maximum of the highway tax at thirty days, was actuated by no other motives than those arising from the public interest. The roads had become so bad a state that without a considerable tax, it would have been impossible to have put them in any kind of repair, and without repairs, in another year, that important road, the turnpike, would have been entirely lost."—Article entitled, " City Affairs," written by the Mayor, John R. Williams, and evidently intended for newspaper publication, September, 1825, " Williams Papers." See also *Detroit Gazette*, August 10, 1824 and July 11, 1825.

[151] *Detroit Gazette*, May 24, 1825.

[152] *Ibid.*, January 1, April 2, 1819; Witherell to his wife, October 29, 1815, " Witherell Papers."

[153] *Detroit Gazette*, May 31, 1822.

[154] *Ibid.*, March 28, April 4, May 9, 1826; *Michigan Herald*, May 10, 1826.

[155] " An Act to alter and establish certain post-roads," " An Act to discontinue certain post-roads and to establish others," March 3, 1823, *United States Statutes at Large*, III, 577-81, 764-68.

[156] For example, wheat was so bulky compared to its value that it could not be transported by land more than a hundred miles at a profit.—F. J. Turner, " The Colonization of the West, 1820-1830," *American Historical Review*, XI (1906), 322.

[157] In New York City a buyer would obtain bids from various shipowners or masters for the transport of his merchandise to Albany. The following is such a bid:

" Hogheads—8/   Casks Nails—1/6
Barrels of all Descriptions—2/   Dry Kegs —1/
Dry goods—6 cts. per cubic foot.   Chests Tea—2/
Tierces—4/

New York, Sept. 23ᵈ 1820. We agree to carry Mr. J. R. Williams freight at the above. [Signed] T. Newton of the Sloop Columbia. To be paid as is customary in the winter."—September 23, 1820, " Williams Papers."

[158] Schoolcraft, *Narrative Journal of Travels . . .* , p. 19. From New York City to Albany the stage fare was $10; the trip usually consumed from three to five days.—Morrison, *op. cit.*, 367.

[159] Thomas, *op. cit.*, p. 36; *Niles' Weekly Register*, January 11, 1817; *Detroit Gazette*, February 11, 1820.

[160] Walker, *op. cit.*, p. 304.

[161] The following table, taken from Schultz, *op. cit.*, II, 12, details the distances, time, and expenses involved in negotiating this route:

	Miles		Days	High Charge	Low Charge
From Albany to					
Schenectady	15	Turnpike Road	½	$ .16 cwt.	$ .16 cwt.
Utica	104	Five and ten ton boats	5	.75	.50
Oswego	104	Five and ten ton boats	3	1.25	1.00
Niagara or Lewiston	172	Schooner	3	.50	.50
Fort Schlosser } and Black Rock ∫	7 17	Level road } Ten ton boat ∫	1½	.25	.25
Totals	419		13	$2.91	$2.41

[162] Colonel William A. Bird, " New York State, Early Transportation," *Buffalo Historical Society, Publications*, II (1880), 24-25.

[163] Receipt, October 23, 1813, invoice, October 26, 1813, Williams to Russel Mathes, November 1, 1813, " Williams Papers."

[164] Watson, *op. cit.*, pp. 414-15. See also Bird, *op. cit.*, pp. 24-25, and Walker, *op. cit.*, pp. 304-05.

[165] Williams to Henry & McKown, May 15, 1817, Williams to Rufus Brown, August 16, 1817, " Williams Letterbook."

[166] Stage coach fare from Albany to Buffalo was about $21.00.—Morrison, *op. cit.*, 367; Crooks to Astor, February 10, 1814, "Ramsay Crooks Papers" (MS, B. H. C.).—In mid-summer, 1815, Witherell journeyed by stage coach from Albany to Buffalo in five days, but he implied that such fast time was exceptional.— Witherell to his wife, August 21, 1815, "Witherell Papers."

[167] *Detroit Gazette*, February 27, 1818.

[168] Thomas, *op. cit.*, p. 36.

[169] For the text of the act authorizing the construction of the canal see Archer Butler Hulbert, *Historic Highways of America* (16 vols. Cleveland, 1902-05), XIV, 219-34. Several essays concerning the events leading to the passage of the legislation and the building of the canal are in the *Buffalo Historical Society, Publications*, II (1880), 227-349.

[170] Hulbert, *op. cit.*, II, p. 116.

[171] *Niles' Weekly Register*, January 11, 1817.

[172] Williams to Samuel Abbott, May (n. d.), 1817, "Williams Papers."

[173] *Detroit Gazette*, November 28, 1817.

[174] Hulbert, *op. cit.*, II, 129, 131; *Detroit Gazette*, January 22, 1819.

[175] *Detroit Gazette*, January 7, 1820.

[176] *Ibid.*, December 7, 1821.

[177] Williams to Boyd & Suydam, February 24, 1822, "Williams Papers."

[178] *Detroit Gazette*, December 7, 1821.

[179] *Ibid.*; Friend Palmer to Mason Palmer, August 7, 1822, "Thomas Palmer Papers" (MS, B. H. C.).

[180] Hulbert, *op. cit.*, II, 135; *Detroit Gazette*, November 22, 1822.

[181] *Detroit Gazette*, May 10, 1825.

[182] *Ibid.*, October 13, 1825.

[183] Horatio G. Spafford, *A Pocket Guide for Tourist and Traveler along the Line of the Canals, and the Interior Commerce of the State of New York* (2nd ed. with additions and corrections, Troy, N. Y., 1825), pp. 32-34.

[184] *Niles' Weekly Register*, November 19, 1825.

[185] *Michigan Herald*, November 8, 1825.

[186] R. J. Meigs to Cass, June 10, 1817, Meigs to James Abbott, June 10, 1817, Carter, *op. cit.*, X, 700-01; Silas Farmer, *The History of Detroit and Michigan, or, The Metropolis Illustrated; A Chronological Cyclopaedia of the Past and Present* . . . (Detroit, 1884), pp. 879-80.

[187] The Detroit mail schedule in 1817 was a follows: "From Detroit by Frenchtown to Fort Meigs once a week, 66 miles. Leave Detroit every Sunday at 9 *a. m.* and arrive at Fort Meigs on Monday by 6 *p. m.* Leave Fort Meigs every Tuesday at 6 *a. m.* and arrive at Detroit on Wednesday by 3 *p. m.*"—Carter, *op. cit.*, X, 700.

[188] *Detroit Gazette*, February 14, 1823.

[189] *Ibid.*, January 24, February 21, 28, 1824.

[190] *Ibid.*, January 24, 1824. The Postal Service asked for bids for carrying the mail between points, usually selling the contract to the private individual whose bid was lowest. In 1820 James Abbott, Postmaster at Detroit, obtained the contract for transporting the mail between Detroit and Fort Meigs with a bid of $500.— James Larned to John Hunt, August 31, 1820, "Charles Larned Papers" (MS, B. H. C.).

[191] *Detroit Gazette*, February 21, December 17, 1824.

[192] Gabriel Richard to Alex Fraser, March 17, 1824, "Gabriel Richard Papers" (Typescript copy, B. H. C.).

[193] *Detroit Gazette*, March 5, 1824.

[194] *Ibid.*, November 12, 1824. In a letter to the editor of the *Gazette* Abbott wrote: "It is proper to inform you that after the current week, the mail for the eastern and southern parts of the Union, will leave this [Detroit] early on Monday and Friday mornings, and will arrive on Wednesdays and Saturdays at 2 P. M."—*Ibid.*, December 3, 1824.

[195] *Ibid.*, December 17, 1824.

CHAPTER III

The Settlement of the Hinterland

Isolated as it was by the difficulties of communication and transportation with the more populous areas of the country, Detroit was further handicapped in recovering from the effects of the war by the total absence of a developed hinterland. Those in authority realized that the future safety and well-being of the city depended upon the celerity with which Michigan Territory could be adjoined, physically and economically, to the rest of the Union. In the opinion of Governor Cass none of the ills afflicting the area were so malignant that they could not be terminated by an injection of new blood and new energy.[1] For a time it appeared that the settlement of the territory would be fairly rapid, for by an act of Congress in 1812, one-third of the six million acres of public land to be granted as military bounties was to be located in Michigan.[2] Shortly after the conclusion of the war, arrangements were perfected for the survey of the Michigan bounty lands.[3] The refusal of the Indians in the region to recognize the validity of the United States' title to the lands delayed the commencement of the surveys.[4] Not until the fall of 1815, after the differences with the Indians had been adjusted, was it possible for the surveyors to begin work.[5] The rain and cold of autumn arrived before much had been accomplished, and in November the surveying parties, worn out by exposure and privation, ceased operations. So disparaging were the reports of the surveyors regarding the quality of Michigan lands that Edward Tiffin, Surveyor-General of the United States, suggested to Josiah Meigs, Commissioner of the General Land Office, that other lands be substituted as bounty lands. He pictured the interior of Michigan as a vast swamp wherein not more than one acre in a thousand would be fit for cultivation. In fact, he declared that the country was not worth the expense of surveying, and he felt that it would be best " to pay off what has been done, and abandon the country." [6] Less than two weeks later in another letter to Meigs he declared: " I am very anxious to hear from you since my representation of Michigan went on. Subsequent accounts confirm the statements, and make the country out worse (if possible) than I had represented it to be." [7] Acting upon the strength of this report, President Madison recommended to Congress that other lands be designated for military bounties in lieu of those in Michigan, and thereupon Congress substituted lands in Illinois. [8]

To those interested in the reconstruction and rehabilitation of the Detroit area, the news of this shift came as a distinct shock. Not only did it put an end to the prospect of an immediate substantial increase in population, but it also spread unfavorable publicity regarding Michigan among those easterners contemplating moving westward. Little could be done to counteract the testimony because of the dearth of information in Detroit concerning the interior. Cass, however, offered rebuttal to the reports of Tiffin, and endeavored to obtain a continuance of the surveys. In a letter to Meigs, May 11, 1816, he declared: " The quality of the land in this territory, I have reason to believe, has been grossly misrepresented. From the report of persons in whom I can place confidence, and from my own observation, I think it will admit a considerable population." In another letter to Meigs, dated the same day, he asserted that the Tiffin report had been

based upon the findings of two surveyors who had arrived in
the territory during the wettest season it had ever experienced,
had stayed but a short time, and had seen only a small portion of it.
To substantiate his position he claimed that two other surveyors
who had been operating in the territory spoke in high terms of
the lands, one of them declaring it to be " the finest country he
ever saw." [9] In answer to a query put to him by Meigs, James
Abbott, Receiver of the Land Office at Detroit, declared that the
lands on the margin of the " principal water courses" were of
good quality, were near the established settlements, and would
probably sell readily.[10] Consequently, in July, 1816 Meigs authorized a resumption of the surveys in areas recommended by Cass
and Abbott in order that the lands situated therein might be
prepared for market.[11]

Following the war the migration of Americans westward began
on a grand scale. An English observer, traveling the National
Road on a journey from Philadelphia to Pittsburgh in 1817, wrote:
" Old America seems to be breaking up, and moving westward.
We are seldom out of sight, as we travel this grand track, of
family groups, behind and before us. . . ." [12] Another traveler
claimed that in the same year, in addition to those traveling by
other means, 20,000 wagons of two-ton capacity crossed the Alle-
ghenies to Pittsburgh. " Nothing has tended so much towards the
rapid progress of the western country," he said, " as the strong
disposition to emigration among the American people themselves.
Even when doing well in the northern, middle, or southern states,
they will break up their establishments, and move westward with
an alacrity and vigor, which no other people would do unless
compelled by necessity." [13] The prospect of fertile lands at low
cost was the great attraction. Tracts of 160 acres of the public
lands could be purchased for two dollars per acre, with a down
payment of one-quarter the purchase price and like payments two,
three, and four years from date. No interest was charged if payments were made promptly, and a discount of 8 per cent was
allowed for cash purchases.[14]

For several years there was small indication in Detroit of the vast westward movement. Easterners preferred lands in the Ohio watershed to those in the land-locked region of the Lakes because of the greater ease of access and the better facilities for transporting produce to market. Thus people in New England crossed the Hudson and followed the Catskill turnpike to the headwaters of the Allegheny, or sailed from Boston for New York, Philadelphia, or Baltimore in order to follow a more southerly route to the lands in the Ohio Valley.[15] Comparative population satistics for 1810 and 1820 illustrate the extent of this migration in the area north of the Ohio River, and its insignificance in Michigan: [16]

	Population 1810	Population 1820
Ohio	230,760	581,534
Indiana	24,520	147,178
Illinois	12,282	55,211
Michigan	4,762	8,896

One of the most favorable portents for Michigan was the conclusion of the treaty with the Indians at the rapids of the Miami late in 1817. Cass, who, with McArthur, negotiated the treaty, wrote to President Monroe:

> We yesterday concluded a treaty with the Indians for nearly all their country within the boundaries of the state of Ohio, for a small portion of the state of Indiana, and for a small portion of the Michigan Territory. . . .

> This acquisition will connect our settlements in this state with those in the territory of Michigan and will enable us to present an iron frontier in the event of any difficulties with the British or Indians in this quarter. . . .

> If we are not deceived in our ideas of the importance of the country, this is by far the most valuable cession, which has been made to the United States at any one time since the Treaty of Greenville in 1795.[17]

The *Detroit Gazette*, which had begun publication only a few months earlier, declared:

> To this territory the purchase is very important, because it connects us with more than a half million of people who inhabit the state of Ohio, and from this day we cease to be an insulated point, insecure and almost inaccessible. We are a constituent part of the American Union. . . .[18]

In his annual message to Congress President Monroe asserted:

> By these acquisitions, and others that may reasonably be expected to follow, we shall be enabled to extend our settlements from the inhabited parts of the state of Ohio along Lake Erie into the Michigan Territory. . . .[19]

The government completed the survey of portions of the public lands in southeastern Michigan by the end of 1817.[20] Agitation began immediately for the sale of these lands. The *Gazette* claimed that people had arrived in the territory to purchase lands, but, " patience exhausted," had purchased lands in Ohio and elsewhere. It added: " Were that almost boundless wilderness, which now approaches within two miles of the city, converted into a farming and manufacturing country, Detroit might challenge competition for extent of commerce and natural advantages, with any of the rising cities of the West." [21] A group of influential Detroit citizens petitioned the President and Congress for an immediate sale of the lands, pointing out that although they had belonged to the United States for some years, not an acre had ever been offered for sale. " The territory abounds," they claimed, " in large tracts of valuable and fertile land, fitted to invite immigrants to the country, and capable of supporting populous and compact settlements." They declared that the settlement of the frontier was the most economical and effective means of safeguarding it, and that people were desirous of moving to Michigan but would not do so until they could purchase lands.

They expressed the belief that ten years after the sale of lands began, Michigan would be ready for statehood.[22] In a letter to Meigs, dated April 3, 1818, Cass declared: "The immediate sale of the public lands in this territory is so important in a national and local point of view that every measure should be adopted, which will facilitate this event. Till then we shall be a dead weight upon the government, remote, exposed and defenseless." [23]

An issue of the *Gazette* of the same date, however, carried the welcome news that later in the year " nearly seventy townships and fractional townships," extending from the River Raisin to the outlet of Lake Huron, would be offered at public auction. " The prospect of the immediate sale of these lands must be gratifying to every citizen," said the editor, " as that event only can insure to this city a permanent prosperity." A month later, " with feelings of the most heartfelt satisfaction," it published the official proclamation of President Monroe, directing the sale of various tracts of public land in Michigan during the next July, September, and November.[24] Resident buyers accounted for most of the purchases during the July sale, for according to the *Gazette* " the current of emigration has not yet been turned towards this territory." The average price at which the lands sold was about four dollars per acre.[25]

The sale of public lands more clearly disclosed the lack of knowledge regarding the interior of Michigan. Nothing of consequence had been done to nullify the testimony of the Tiffin report. Descriptions of the lands dealt with generalities and were based largely upon hearsay evidence.[26] A contributor to the *Gazette*, signing himself " A Stranger," wrote:

> Before the building of the steamboat on Lake Erie, little more was known in the Atlantic states of this territory, than [that] Detroit and Mackinac belonged to it. . . . It is truly a subject of regret, that nine-tenths of the strangers who visit this delightful section of our country, should go home without being able to answer one single question correctly, re-

specting the interior. . . . It is truly a matter of astonishment
that many of the citizens of Detroit, who have resided here
for forty years and upwards, should be profoundly ignorant
of the country twenty miles back from the river. How, then,
could it be expected that those of us who live a thousand
miles off should be undeceived? [27]

Indians and Indian traders, more acquainted with the interior,
probably kept their knowledge a secret—if they did not describe
it falsely—in order that their way of life might be preserved.[28]

Much of the land purchased at the Detroit sales in 1818 was
for speculative purposes. This led to a search for the best lands
by individuals or groups of individuals possessed of the means
to purchase large tracts.[29] In the fall of 1818 an expedition consisting of competent Detroit citizens, including the Protestant
clergyman, set out to explore the lands north of the city. They
penetrated the wilderness to a point several miles north of the
present city of Pontiac, and after an absence of twelve days
returned to Detroit with a report that was in surprising contrast
to what was ordinarily believed in regard to the country.[30] It
included " the most glowing and flattering accounts of a country
of the choicest land, generally undulating," and requiring " nothing but the vigorous arm of industry to convert it into the granary
of America." [31] Subsequent explorations added to the knowledge
of lands near Detroit, and confirmed their agricultural possibilities.[32]

Although the land sales in 1818 failed to add much to the
population of the area, they served to mark a turning point in its
history. Elkanah Watson predicted that the sales would " give
new wings to the progress and population of the country." [33]
The *Gazette* reviewed the catastrophes that had befallen the city
in the past, and proclaimed: " From this summer past, we may
date the era of our prosperity." [34] Fourteen years later, in an
address before the Michigan Historical Society, John Biddle
reviewed the course of events and substantiated this prediction:

As an American community founding its prosperity upon the permanent resources of its own industry, Michigan may date its origin from the year 1818; and if the original forest had then covered the shores of the Detroit River, there are grounds, at least plausible, for the supposition that they might at this moment have exhibited a higher degree of improvement than that which we now witness.[35]

This latter contention was based upon the agricultural inaptitude of the *habitants* who made up the greater part of the population of the area and who owned most of the lands in the vicinity of Detroit. The continued dependence upon Ohio and other states for foodstuffs was irksome to the more progressive American element, for it tended to maintain the high cost of living in the city.[36] The sale of public land opened the way for the hundreds of American farmers that the *Gazette* estimated were necessary to supply the wants of the townspeople, the garrison, and the fur traders and fishermen.[37]

Before the tide of western migration could be inclined toward Michigan, it was necessary to acquaint the East with the advantages of its situation and with the newly acquired information regarding its lands. Other prejudices remained to be overcome. For years the rumor had been prevalent in the East that the climate of the Detroit region was unhealthy, and this feeling was probably strengthened somewhat by the deaths of hundreds of soldiers from disease at Detroit during the fall and winter of 1813.[38] Fear of Indian hostility also served to retard the ingress of settlers; still another check was the undemocratic nature of the government of the territory, ruled as it was by the Governor and Judges, and without representation in Congress.[39]

The *Detroit Gazette* was undoubtedly the most potent medium for dispensing information relative to the territory. It began publication on July 25, 1817 at the suggestion and under the patronage of Governor Cass.[40] Its importance in publicizing the attractions of Michigan was far greater than its small circulation would indicate.[41] Papers having a national circulation, such as the *Niles' Weekly Register* and the *National Intelligencer*, reprinted articles taken from the *Gazette*. It claimed: "Almost every thing which appears in our paper, relating to the geography, topography, mineralogy, or history of this portion of the country is published in numerous papers thro'out the Union."[42] In the years that followed, the paper continued to champion the character of Michigan, utilizing every opportunity to promote its welfare and offering able rebuttal to derogatory opinions concerning it.

The reports of Evans, Darby, and Watson, who visited Detroit in 1818, were effective in creating more favorable impressions of the territory. Evans dwelt at length upon its attractions and the fine quality of its lands. He disclaimed that a speculative interest in them prompted his remarks and declared:

> I deem it my duty to express a high opinion of the Michigan Territory, because facts warrant such a course, and it is important that those of my fellow citizens, who may be disposed to emigrate to the west, should possess every information upon the subject. . . .
>
> In traveling more than four thousand miles in the western parts of the United States, I met no tract of country which, upon the whole, impressed my mind so favorably as the Michigan Territory. Erroneous ideas have heretofore been entertained respecting this territory. . . .
>
> The soil is generally fertile, and a considerable proportion of it is very rich. Its climate is delightful; and its situation novel and interesting. . . . There is no place in the world more healthy than the city of Detroit. . . . A yankee farmer carrying with him to this place his knowledge of agriculture, and his industry, might soon acquire a very handsome estate.[43]

Darby wrote in regard to the area:

> Though the soil is good in general, some of it excellent, and all parts well situated for agriculture and commerce,

some causes have hitherto operated to prevent any serious emigration to the Michigan Territory.[44]

Watson, a contemporary authority upon agriculture, commented:

> Blessed with a luxuriant soil and with the highest conveniences of water intercourse and occupying a central attitude upon the most extensive internal navigation by inland seas on earth, what may not Michigan aspire to become? . . . The presence of a new and different class of farmers, more enlightened, more industrious and progressive, would at once give to it a new aspect.[45]

The arrival of new settlers in Michigan, however, was painfully slow. Darby claimed that during a month-long journey from Geneva, New York to Detroit he encountered hundreds moving to the West, but " not one in fifty with an intention to settle in Michigan Territory." [46] In May, 1818 a citizens' committee took steps to publicize the territory, and raised a sum of money to finance the campaign.[47] Although the results were meager there appeared to be confidence that the situation would improve, for thirty new buildings were erected during the summer.[48] In the fall of 1818 the *Gazette* announced that several parties were investigating the interior and selecting farms, and that others had already begun to improve the lands which they had purchased.[49]

The formation of the Pontiac Land Company at this time was probably the most significant move in promoting interior settlement. As a speculative venture a group of Detroit citizens purchased a tract of 1,280 acres situated about twenty-five miles north of the city in the area recently explored. The village of Pontiac was laid out on a plat of 160 acres. Lots in the town were offered for sale while the remainder of the acreage was divided into farms. To make the project more attractive to the prospective settler, the company erected a sawmill, a grist-mill, and a blacksmith shop, all of which were in operation by the fall of 1819.[50]

In addition to these improvements the Territorial Legislature approved the construction of a road through the area,[51] and commissioners appointed for the purpose decided upon Pontiac as the seat of justice in Oakland County.[52] The venture won the approval of the *Gazette*:

> By associations, such as the Pontiac company, much good can be done, and many facilities afforded to the settlement of this territory, which could not be embraced in the exertions of the individuals not acting in concert. Mills, which may be considered as the buds which bloom into villages in new countries, can soon be erected, purchases liberally credited, and the mechanic and farmer better encouraged and supported.[53]

The high prices paid for produce in Detroit during the winter of 1818-1819 led the *Gazette* to plead once again for New England farmers to settle in Michigan. It claimed that a farmer " of common industry and enterprise could purchase one or two good farms with the avails of his barn yard and vegetable patch for one year." It called upon " friends of this territory . . . to disseminate knowledge of its general and peculiar advantages," and promised that those who should come would " become independently rich in a short time." [54] When the rumor began that the military forces stationed in the city were to be removed, it protested vehemently. In the past it had urged it readers to write to their friends in the East and attempt to nullify the false impressions prevailing there in regard to the dangers from Indians.[55] If eight or ten hundred farmers settled in Michigan they would secure the territory so effectively that there would be no need of a garrison, but if the military force was removed the *Gazette* felt that the defenseless state of the area would check immigration. Besides, the federal monies expanded for the support of the military department were necessary to the welfare of the territory, and if deprived of this resource, it would be less attractive to the prospective settler.[56]

In the spring of 1819 newcomers arrived from the state of New York, and began to take up lands within twenty and thirty miles of Detroit. The *Gazette* also received the " vivifying intelligence " that many other farmers from that state and from other parts of the Union were making ready to remove to Michigan during the summer. It cautioned the citizens to remember that the future of the territory depended upon its recognition as a healthy farming country, and it urged that selfish speculative interests be subordinated in order that the new farmers could be directed to the best lands on the market.[57] By summer, however, the nation-wide economic depression had dampened these hopes— and few new settlers arrived.[58]

Nevertheless, the surveys of the public lands in Michigan were continued. In the summer of 1819 a veteran surveyor, operating in the region of the River Raisin, wrote to an acquaintance: " I have the satisfaction to state to you and your friends at Detroit, that I have just surveyed the best tract of country that I ever surveyed in my life, either of private or public lands." [59] In the spring of 1820 it was announced that the lands in eighteen additional townships would be offered for sale the following summer. The *Gazette* claimed that there was no better land in the United States, and urged those people residing in New York and New England who were desirous of migrating to Michigan to appoint agents to select their lands.[60]

Meanwhile, in the fall of 1819 Cass negotiated a treaty with the Chippewa Indians whereby the United States gained title to a vast tract of land in the central part of Michigan and in the Saginaw Bay region.[61] By this purchase an extension of the frontier was assured and the fear of Indian disturbance lessened. Since Detroit was the logical *entrepot* for these lands, its citizens eagerly anticipated their settlement and development.

Cass left Detroit in the spring of 1820, accompanied by Schoolcraft and several other men of scientific background, to explore the northwestern part of Michigan and the Lake Superior region.

The expedition, which was sponsored by the War Department, studied the topography of the country, made maps, and investigated reports of mineral deposits. It also examined the situation of the Indians in the area and sought to determine their attitude regarding the sale of their lands. The northward course of the expedition followed the eastern shore of the territory, thus making it possible for the members to gather more information concerning the lands purchased in 1819.[62] Cass returned to Detroit in September, traveling overland from Chicago through the rich lands in western Michigan still in the possession of the Indians. The results of the expedition were highly favorable to the territory. Its official nature lent credence to its findings and brought the whole area into public notice. It revealed the richness of the agricultural and mineral resources to be found there, and the fine possibilities for commercial and industrial enterprise. When Schoolcraft's account of the expedition was published in Albany in 1821, public interest in the discoveries had mounted to such a degree that the entire edition sold in a month—some copies even finding their way to Europe.[63]

The economic depression of 1819 demonstrated certain faults in the accepted method of marketing public lands. In the first place the liberal credit system encouraged speculation. Consequently, much of the best land was purchased by groups of individuals who had no intention of developing it, but who hoped to sell it to others at a profit. Secondly, the smallest tract of land that could be purchased was 160 acres. This worked a hardship on the farmer of small means who had little capital after removing to the West. Since the first few years were spent in clearing the land and improving it, he had difficulty in producing enough to meet his yearly payments.[64] In Detroit this problem was aggravated by the scarcity of money in circulation, for land purchases had drained most of it from the region.[65] When the depression began in 1819, the price of produce fell to such a low level that farmers throughout the West who had purchased on credit were faced with the prospect of forfeiting their lands and improvements for want of ability to meet their annual installments.[66] Indeed, the situation had become so serious by 1820 that Congress found it necessary to suspend forfeitures for one year to save the West from ruin.[67]

Shortly thereafter, it passed legislation revising the procedure for selling the public lands. Effective July 1, 1820, all sales were to be on a cash basis. The price of land was reduced to $1.25 per acre, and the minimum purchase, from 160 acres to 80.[68] Thus for the sum of $100.00 an eastern farmer could purchase a small tract of western land and settle on it without fear of foreclosure. In order to relieve those who had purchased lands prior to this change, Congress acted in March, 1821 to permit those in default to relinquish a part of their holdings and have the ensuing credit applied to the lands which they retained in lieu of scheduled cash payments.[69]

The new system was effective in promoting the settlement of Michigan. This was evidenced by the returns at the Land Office in Detroit during the following years. During the month of July, 1820 when the cash system went into operation, receipts for land amounted to $832.58. In June, 1821, however, they rose to $2,304.22, and in June, 1822 to $5,162.91. The *Gazette* declared that it had heard of no purchases for speculative purposes, and that nearly every quarter-section had been taken up by practical farmers. It estimated that not more than five farmers in a hundred in Michigan held their lands under the credit system.[70]

The success of the Pontiac Company in promoting the settlement of Oakland County induced a group of Detroit citizens to plan a similar venture in the area south of Saginaw Bay. Rivers originating there were tributary to the Saginaw River, thus offering water communication with the Great Lakes. The group organized the Sciawassa Company and invited participation in the enterprise at $50.00 per share. It proposed to lay out a town near the headwaters of the rivers and to promote the settlement of an area forty miles square. Since the lands were not yet offered for sale, and since little was known regarding them, the company outfitted an exploring party to select the site of the town and to examine the soil, waterways, mill sites, and resources of the whole area.[71] The exploration was not as extensive as contemplated, for provisions ran low, but after an absence of more than three weeks, the party returned to Detroit with high praise of the country it had visited. A detailed journal of the expedition appeared in successive numbers of the *Gazette*.[72] Although the company apparently was thwarted in its plans to settle the country, it was influential in clearing up false impressions in the East regarding Michigan lands.[73] Some of the lands acquired by the Treaty of Saginaw were placed on the market in 1822.[74]

By 1821 the settlement of southern Michigan had progressed to such an extent that the United States took measures to purchase additional lands from the Indians. Once again Cass was commissioned to negotiate with them. On August 29, 1821, he and Sibley, the other commissioner, affixed their signatures to the Treaty of Chicago, whereby the United States gained title to approximately five million acres of land. Except for a few reservations, the Indians ceded all of their lands in Michigan south of the Grand River, and granted right of way for roads from Fort Wayne and Detroit to Chicago.[75] Cass was conscious of the worth of the lands purchased as he had traversed them on the last leg of his expedition in 1820. Williams, who attended the Treaty council at Chicago in order to sell merchandise, said of the newly-purchased lands:

> It is unquestionably one of the finest tracts of country I ever traversed and will at no very distant period become very abundant and productive as it is of that description to require but a few years settlement and little labor to give it the appearance of an old settlement from the natural facilities and advantages which it affords and unites.[76]

With this acquisition the United States obtained possession of a total of seventeen and a half million acres of land in Michigan Territory, two and a quarter millions of which had been surveyed by 1821.[77] The prospective development of this vast hinterland augured well for Detroit, promising an early fulfillment of School-craft's prediction on visiting the city in 1820: " It is destined to be to the regions of the northwest what St. Louis is rapidly becoming in the southwest, the seat of its commerce, the repository of its wealth, and the grand focus of its moral, political, and physical energies." [78]

With the increase in population of the shorelands, new counties were established and organized in Michigan Territory. By proclamation, Cass established Monroe County in 1817, Macomb in 1818, and St. Clair in 1820. The successful promotions by the Pontiac Company led to the establishment of Oakland, the first inland county, in 1819, and its organization the following year. In order to clarify the boundaries of the established counties, Cass redefined them in 1822 in line with the public surveys. At the same time he laid out and defined the boundaries of six new counties, Lapeer, Sanilac, Saginaw, Shiawassee, Washtenaw, and Lenawee.[79] These were established before their lands were occupied ". . . to prevent those collisions of interest and opinion, which generally attend the laying out of counties after a country is settled, and to hold out inducements to migration and enterprise, by the establishment of counties in every part of the territory. . . ." [80]

By February, 1821 " about two hundred " families were living in Oakland County, whereas only four families were living there two years earlier. Sixty-three sleighs, loaded with wheat, arrived at the mill in Pontiac in one week from points more than twenty-five miles distant.[81] Eastern prejudices regarding the territory were diminishing, and as the true knowledge of its lands became more general, the demand for them increased. The rapid progress of the Erie Canal added to their attractiveness. Illustrative of this change of attitude, the *Niles' Weekly Register* said:

The time is about to arrive when a journey to that city
[Detroit] will become a jaunt of pleasure through the Erie
Canal and a steamboat voyage on that lake; and Michigan, yet
thinly populated, teem with busy men, employed in the works
of agriculture and art. It is a fine country and, though so
much neglected in times past, will hereafter draw off a large
portion of the emigration from the old states.[82]

A partial recovery from the economic distress pervading the nation
was indicated by the rise in the price of wheat in 1821. Although
it could have little effect upon the income of the farmers of
Michigan, the *Gazette* felt it would stimulate emigration to the
territory.

In apparent confirmation of this viewpoint settlers began arriving in increased numbers in the spring of 1822. "From all
accounts," said the *Gazette*, "the *current of emigration* has taken
the course which the wishes of our fellow-citizens have long since
designated." [83] By June the influx of new settlers was so great that
it was "difficult to ascertain, with any degree of certainty, their
actual numbers." Many of the new arrivals were from Vermont,
Massachusetts, and Pennsylvania, and a few were from Ohio; but
the majority were from New York, for according to the *Gazette*,
"in that great state this territory *begins* to be known." Many
of the newcomers had sent agents to appraise the lands in Michigan before setting out, and the arrival of numerous others "to
see the country" convinced the *Gazette* that "the barriers to
emigration" were giving way, and that a "tide" had begun to
flow which nothing could retard.[84] Some of the agents made
thorough explorations of the interior and communicated their
findings in detail to their friends in the East.[85] Citizens of Monroe
offered free transportation to homeseekers wishing to view the
lands in the neighborhood of the River Raisin.[86]

Indicative of the extent of the migration, the receipts at the
Detroit Land Office in October, 1822 were 13 per cent greater
than in June.[87] During the ensuing winter a number of families

arrived in the city, some coming by sleigh across Canada and others by wagon from the south, the latter avoiding the Black Swamp by journeying on the frozen waters of Lake Erie.[88]

In those areas of the West which had been settled earlier the value of both unimproved and improved property had increased to such an extent that it was beyond the reach of easterners of limited means. To many of these, however, this illustrated the expediency of purchasing and improving public land.[89] Michigan offered a rich field for endeavor. Its advantages were set forth by the *New York Spectator* in its issue of March 4, 1823:

> When we contemplate the numerous advantages which this territory possesses, in respect of soil, climate, interior streams, and its situation as to a market for its productions, we are led to the belief that its settlement and prosperity will increase as rapidly as any portion of the new country, within the boundaries of the United States. Perhaps no stronger argument can be urged in support of this belief than merely to state the fact, that a barrel of potashes, flour, or other produce, can be transported from Detroit to Buffalo, with as little expense through Lake Erie, as a like quantity can be transported by land, in the western part of this state, to the canal, from places which lie twenty-five or thirty miles from the canal route. Again: The public land in the vicinity of Detroit can be purchased for $1 and twenty-five cents per acre—those in the western part of this state lying twenty-five or thirty miles from the route of the canal, are valued from ten to twenty dollars per acre. This brief view is sufficient to convince any one of the value of the lands in Michigan Territory now in market, and of the certainty that they will rapidly increase in value.[90]

The first settlers arriving in the spring reported that many others in New York were making ready to move to Michigan.[91] A few weeks later the *Buffalo Journal* observed: " For a few days past our wharves and taverns have been literally thronged with people emigrating to this new country [Michigan], nearly all of

whom appear to belong to the most valuable class of settlers—
practical farmers, of moderate capital and good habits." [92] The
number of land sales at Detroit in May, 1823 were seven times
greater than in the same month of previous years.[93] The activity
of the Land Office in Detroit,[94] and the wide extent of territory
it serviced induced Congress to authorize the opening of an additional one in Michigan.[95] It was established at Monroe in the
spring of 1823.[96]

The extent of the migration to Michigan convinced the editor
of the *Gazette* that the necessity of combatting misrepresentations
and prejudices regarding the territory had ended.[97] In fact, by
the end of the year he was of the belief that the false impression
created by the reports of the surveyors was, on the whole, " a most
fortunate circumstance " for the territory. If Michigan lands had
been given as bounties to soldiers, eastern capitalists would have
gained possession of large tracts, and would have held them for
speculative purposes. To them the occupants would have been
forced to pay tribute " in the shape of rent." Nor was settlement
impeded by the refusal of large land-owners to market their
holdings until the surrounding area had greatly increased in value.
As events transpired, Michigan was settling rapidly; in almost
every instance, the newcomers owned the land they occupied—
which was seldom more than a section.[98]

The lands south and west of Detroit began to attract a larger
portion of the new settlers by 1824. Washtenaw County, established in 1822, was the seventh to be organized in a period of
four years, and the commissioners appointed to select the site
of a county seat spoke highly of its lands.[99] The villages of
Ypsilanti and Ann Arbor were laid out, the latter being designated
as the county seat.[100] Although there were but nine people living
in the county in July, 1823, in 1824 seventy-nine people at the
" lower settlement " and about fifty at the " upper settlement "
attended Independence Day celebrations.[101] Monroe County, which
had settled slowly, attracted more settlers after the opening of
the Land Office at its county seat. Explorations conducted in the

upper regions of the River Raisin demonstrated the worth of the lands there and led to the founding of Tecumseh in Lenawee County.[102]

Northeast of Detroit the villages of Mt. Clemens and St. Clair were laid out in 1818, and became the county seats of Macomb and St. Clair counties, respectively.[103] Much of the land around Mt. Clemens had been purchased by speculators, whose demands were sufficiently high to drive prospective settlers to the cheaper public lands. The St. Clair region settled even more slowly because it was somewhat removed from the direct line of western migration, and was densely forested. A contributing factor was the circulation of false reports by promoters of other areas that the region was swampy and bred deadly fevers.[104]

During the winter of 1823-24 families continued to arrive from New York through Canada. A large number of " land hunters " also journeyed by way of " the tedious and expensive land route." [105] By Presidential proclamation those lands returned to the United States according to provisions of the act to relieve purchasers who acquired lands under the credit system were to be offered for sale the first Monday in June, 1824. Lands forfeited for non-payment were to be sold at the same time, as were the lands in eighteen townships in the area immediately northwest of Wayne County. On the first Monday in July the lands in twenty-one additional townships were to be marketed. Much to the dismay of the *Gazette*, however, the federal government, evidently as an economy measure, discontinued the advertising of the land sales in all those newspapers authorized to publish the laws of the United States, inserting them only in the *National Intelligencer* and a paper in Batavia, New York. In order to obtain more publicity for the sales, the *Gazette* suggested that Detroiters subscribe to a fund to publish the proclamation in several newspapers in the northern and eastern states.[106] It protested, too, the discontinuance of surveys in the territory for the year, claiming that it would keep some of the best land out of market for a year or two longer. The situation was even more aggravating in that there were arriving daily in Michigan settlers who wished to purchase lands in the unsurveyed regions.[107]

Despite these apparent discouragements, the steamboat and sailing vessels landed pioneer families in ever-increasing numbers. Land sales increased accordingly. On May 17, 1824 more than one and a half times as much land was sold at the Detroit office alone as was sold in the whole territory during the year 1820.[108] The total land sold at the two offices in 1824 was more than four times that of 1822.[109] Extensive sales were made in every part of the territory that had been surveyed, which indicated, according to the register of the Land Office at Detroit, "that every part of the country abounds in land of the best quality. . . ." [110] During the winter of 1824-25 advertisements appeared in newspapers in western New York announcing the formation of companies for the purpose of removing to Michigan. Said the *Gazette*: " Success *will* attend them." [111]

In the spring of 1825 the opening of the Erie Canal was no longer a distant reality. Only a few miles remained to be completed, and the many miles that had been opened for service had substantially reduced the cost of the long journey from New England and New York to Detroit. Schoolcraft wrote about this time:

> It is among the anomalies of history, that a country deemed so inaccessible from swamps in 1818, as to be unfit to be given in bounty lands to the soldiers of the late army, should, within six years thereafter, be found to possess qualities of so different a nature, as to attract crowds of emigrants from the fertile banks of the Genesee, and to divert, in a measure, the current of migration from the Wabash and the Illinois. Time, better means of comparison, and the spirit of exploration, which characterizes the present era, without showing the advantages of other parts of the western country to be less than has been claimed for them, have, at the same time, shown the advantages of Michigan Territory to be in many respects equal:—while its vicinity to the parent settlements, and the

ease and cheapness of access, together with the quality of the
land and the permanent benefits anticipated from the completion of the Erie Canal, give it, in the minds of many, a
superiority.[112]

On the average the steamboat landed more than three hundred
passengers weekly at Detroit, the great majority of whom were
new settlers.[113] " Our most sanguine expectations in relation to
the settlement of this fine country," said the *Gazette*, " are more
than realized." [114] So great was the influx that it was difficult to
find accommodations in the city for the newcomers; and citizens
opened their homes to strangers when the " public houses " were
filled.[115] By the end of June, when the usual slackening of immigration set in, the *Gazette* estimated that not less than three
thousand new arrivals had landed in Detroit during the spring,
while many others had landed at other ports or had journeyed
to the territory by land. A 50 per cent increase in population of
Michigan was predicted for the year. At the Detroit Land Office
47,052 acres of land were marketed between the first of May and
the last of June. " Any one who has a curiosity to see the forest
visibly moving before the arm of improvement," said the *Gazette*,
" will do well to make a trip from Pontiac to the settlements on
the Rouge, from thence down the Huron to Woodruff's Grove." [116]

The settlement of the lands west of Detroit was stimulated by
the act of Congress providing for the survey and laying out of a
military road from Detroit to Chicago.[117] The reports of surveyors
praised the lands in the vicinity of the headwaters of the St. Joseph
River—near which the Chicago Road would pass.[118] Speculators
immediately began purchasing tracts of land along the proposed
route, and groups of homeseekers followed its blazes to the southwest.[119]

The arrival of new settlers in Detroit, which had practically
ceased during the harvest months, took on such vigor in the fall
that again " the taverns in town and country " were " filled to over-
flowing." The great majority of the two hundred and fifty new-

comers arriving in Detroit weekly continued to come from western
New York, but some were from other states; and, according to
the *Gazette*, they were "excellent emigrants" and "calculated
well to make a new country rich and powerful by their intelligence, enterprise, and capital."[120]

Oakland County contained "between three and four thousand
inhabitants" by the end of 1825, while Washtenaw laid claim to
a population of from fifteen hundred to two thousand—two-thirds
of which had been added during the year. Macomb County, situated east of the course of the migration, settled more slowly.[121]
The growing popularity of Monroe County may be judged by the
fact that the population of the town of Monroe increased one-
third during the year.[122] Other counties whose lands had been
deemed unfit for agriculture a few years earlier had received their
first settlers, and more newcomers were industriously exploring
them in the search of homesteads.[123]

Detroit, the port of entry for the majority of the new settlers,
benefitted by its situation as the western terminus of steamboat
navigation and as the gateway to the new country. Consequently,
"it became a rendezvous for settlers and a clearing house of ideas
about the interior." Immigrants intending to settle elsewhere in
the northwest made only tentative plans until they reached Detroit; frequently, upon their arrival, they were induced to settle
in its environs or in nearby regions.[124] Whereas at the end of
1818 the population of the city was 1,110, by the end of 1823
it had risen to 1,325. With 500 more inhabitants "living directly
in the vicinity," plus the 81 soldiers and their families "in the
cantonment," Detroit laid claim to "a gross population of 2000
souls."[125] So extensive was the increase in the next two years
that by the end of 1825 the inhabitants within the bounds of
the city probably totaled 2,000.[126]

Despite the increase in the population of Detroit, the interior
of Wayne County attracted few settlers. This was due, for the
most part, to the low, swampy character of the land back of the

city. Detroit was located on a water-laid moraine, a broad clay ridge of slight relief and gentle slopes. The land was heavily timbered—which made it less desirable to the new settler than the more open land found in neighboring counties. Much of the soil was " lake clay," which was " sticky and tenacious," but when wet was " easily worked to a soft plastic mass." The flatness of the region prevented adequate drainage, and the heavy forests retarded evaporation by the sun and wind. For at least four months of the year the area was covered with ponds and marshes, and it was this region which had to be crossed in going to the west and northwest of Detroit that led travelers and surveyors to claim that the territory was unfit for cultivation.[127] The sluggishness of the streams flowing through the plain held no incentive for the settler wishing to locate in a region affording mill facilities.[128] In 1825 a committee of local citizens studied the possibilities of improving transportation through the area by digging a network of canals to connect with the streams in the higher regions. The committee reported in favor of the project, pointing out that in addition to providing an avenue to the interior, it would drain the swamp lands back of the city, would furnish water for hydraulic purposes, and would place the city within reach of an adequate supply of firewood. In addition, the earth dug from the canal would form the foundation of a good turnpike road.[129] In all probability the expense of the enterprise was too great for the territory, and the increasing activity of the government in sanctioning military roads in Michigan probably ended it.

A few venturesome settlers had located in the townships of Farmington, Livonia, and Nankin by 1824, and in the same year the first purchases were made in the township of Plymouth. Located in the northwest corner of Wayne County, this latter township contained higher lands within its bounds. A branch of the Rouge River was sufficiently rapid to furnish some water power. In the spring of 1825 several pioneer families arrived in Detroit from the East and journeyed by ox-cart to the heights at Plymouth, thus initiating the settlement of the interior of the county.[130]

In 1806, shortly after fire had destroyed the old town of Detroit, Congress granted a tract of 10,000 acres of land to the stricken frontier settlement to defray the cost of constructing a new court house and jail. The Governor and Judges were charged with the responsibility of marketing the lands and managing the proceeds. A portion of this tract was surveyed into small parcels and auctioned in 1809. It was north of the northern boundary of the town, however; and, at the time, there was small demand for acreage located so far from the river.[131] The turmoil precipitated by the War of 1812 caused such a confused state of affairs in the town that sales in the tract were suspended. With the coming of peace Cass was anxious to place the lands in the tract on the market, but all records pertaining to it had been destroyed or carried away during the enemy occupation. He managed to secure duplicates, however, and by June, 1816 had been instrumental in having the tract surveyed into plots of 80 and 160 acres.[132] In that month it was announced that 9,056 acres of the lands would be offered at public auction the following September. John R. Williams wrote the announcement proclaiming the sale:

> To practical husbandmen, never was a more advantageous opportunity offered, for making a profitable and agreeable settlement. The lands are generally of rich soil, well timbered, and adapted to the cultivation of all kinds of grain, hay and vegetables. The importance of the article of fire wood so near a growing city needs no comment, and the high prices of all kinds of country produce, hay and vegetables in this country requires only to be known to engage and secure the attention of industrious agriculturists.
>
> The whole of said tract of land is situated within from two to four miles from the flourishing city of Detroit. . . . The titles to purchasers will come directly from the Governor and Judges of the Territory of Michigan. . . .[133]

The marshy character of much of the land, however, belied this description,[134] and few purchases were made, for two years later more than 8,300 acres remained to be sold.[135] Despite the increase in the population that followed the first sales of public land in Michigan, and despite the fact that the turnpike road leading to Pontiac passed directly through it, in 1823 most of the acreage was still in the hands of the Governor and Judges. A growing demand for a realization of the terms of the grant led to an arrangement whereby all of the remainder of the tract, including the city lots that had been carved from it, was turned over to private contractors as compensation for the erection of a " Court House or Capitol in the city of Detroit." [136] The new owners immediately offered " 6,640 acres of land and 144 city lots " for sale, and advertised that carpenters, joiners, masons, stonecutters, boatmen, cartmen, and day-laborers would be given land for their labors.[137] One hundred and twenty-four five-acre " wood lots " were offered for sale in the hope that the high price of firewood in the city would attract purchasers.[138] The area had attracted few actual settlers, however, by the end of 1825.

With the settlement of the hinterland and the extension of the frontier the need of a military establishment at Detroit diminished. By 1817 the personnel of the garrison numbered but four hundred.[139] Although it had protested the removal of United States troops in 1819, the *Gazette* termed the action " judicious " in 1823. It felt, however, that adequate forces should be maintained along the straits to assure their protection.[140] Less than a hundred soldiers were in the garrison at the end of the year.[141] About this time the citizens of Detroit initiated a campaign for a federal grant of the military reservation located within the environs of the city. " In its present situation it is of little use," said the *Gazette*, " and as there is a great probability that Detroit will not soon become a military post of any consequence, two-thirds of this reservation could at this time be disposed of without injury to the public service." It recommended that the United States make a gift of the reservation to the city to compensate it for sums expended in the past for the support of sick and destitute soldiers discharged from service. With the proceeds from the sale of the lands a hospital and poorhouse might be erected.[142] A portion of the reserve was turned over to the city in the spring of 1824,[143] but efforts continued to obtain the remainder.[144] In the spring of 1826 Congress granted the remaining lands to Detroit with the provision that the city build a magazine for federal stores outside its limits.[145]

Thus, after a century and a quarter of military occupation, Detroit was without a garrison. The alacrity with which the citizens acquiesced to the evacuation was an indication of the increased strength of the area. No longer were federal expenditures of vital necessity to the welfare of the city, as they had been in the past, for its new economy was founded upon the resources of the developing hinterland.

Meanwhile, the United States had been active in clearing up the titles to lands in the region. Various land boards had met during the years to investigate claims in accordance with several acts of Congress, and by 1825 the maze of divergent titles had been solved.[146]

CHAPTER III—NOTES

[1] Cass to Josiah Meigs, May 11, 1816; Woodbridge to Meigs, May, 1815, Clarence Edwin Carter, ed. and comp., *The Territorial Papers of the United States* (10 vols. Washington, 1934-1942), X, 633-36, 544-45.

[2] " An Act to provide for designating, surveying and granting the Military Bount Lands," May 6, 1812, United States, *The Statutes at Large of the United States* . . *Concurrent Resolutions, Recent Treaties, Conventions and Executive Proclamation* (55 vols.; Boston, 1845-73, Washington, 1875-1942), II, 728-30. (Hereafter cited as *United States Statutes at Large.*)

[3] Meigs to James Madison, March 6, 1815, Edward Tiffin to Meigs, March 1815, Meigs to Tiffin, March 13, 1815, Meigs to Cass, March 22, 1815, Meigs t Tiffin, March 27, 1815, " Contract between Edward Tiffin and Alexander Holmes, April 18, 1815, Carter, *op. cit.,* X, 514-15, 516-17, 518-19, 520, 526-27, 527-30.

[4] Woodbridge to Meigs, May, 1815, Tiffin to Meigs, June 12, 1815, Benjami Hough to Tiffin, June 12, 1815, Meigs to Madison, June 20, 1815, Carter, *op. cit* X, 544-45, 549-50, 550-54, 554.

[5] Cass to Tiffin, September 4, 1815, Carter, *op. cit.,* X, 594-95.

[6] Tiffin to Meigs, December 11, 1815, *American State Papers, Public Lands* (38 vols.; Washington, 1832-1861), III, 164-65.

[7] Tiffin to Meigs, December 11, 1815, *American State Papers, Public Lands*, III, 165.

[8] James D. Richardson, comp., *A Compilation of the Messages and Papers of the Presidents* (11 vols.; n. p., 1913), I, 555-56; "An Act to authorize the survey of two millions of acres of the public lands, in lieu of that quantity heretofore authorized to be surveyed, in the Territory of Michigan as military bounty lands," April 29, 1816, *United States Statutes at Large*, III, 332.

[9] Carter, *op. cit.*, X, 634-36.

[10] Abbott to Meigs, June 30, 1816, *ibid.*, X, 655-57.

[11] Meigs to Cass, July 16, 1816, Meigs to Tiffin, Carter, *op. cit.*, X, 659.

[12] Morris Birkbeck, *Notes on a Journey in America, from the Coast of Virginia to the Territory of Illinois* (London, 1818), p. 25. Birkbeck had been commissioned by a group of fellow Englishmen who were interested in emigrating to America to investigate western lands. His reports to his friends constitute an interesting commentary upon conditions in America in 1817.

[13] Daniel Blowe, *A Geographical, Commercial, and Agricultural View of the United States of America, Forming a Complete Emigrant's Directory throughout Every Part of the Republic, Particularly the Western States and Territories* (Liverpool, 1819), p. 63.

[14] Thomas Donaldson, *The Public Domain* (Washington, 1884), p. 204.

[15] Frederick Turner, "The Colonization of the West, 1820-1830," *American Historical Review*, XI (1906), 311.

[16] United States, *Fifth Census; or, Enumeration of the Inhabitants of the United States, 1830, to Which is Prefixed a Schedule of the Whole Number of Persons Within the Several Districts of the United States, Taken According to the Acts of 1790, 1800, 1810, 1820* (Washington, 1832), pp. 26-27.

[17] Cass to Monroe, September 30, 1817, "Lewis Cass Papers" (MS, Burton Historical Collection, Detroit Public Library; hereafter cited as B. H. C.).

[18] *Detroit Gazette*, October 3, 1817.

[19] Richardson, *op. cit.*, I, 585.

[20] *Detroit Gazette*, March 13, 1818. While the surveyors had experienced difficulties in completing their tasks, they had evidently turned in better reports concerning the quality of Michigan lands, for Tiffin informed Meigs: "there will be a good deal of excellent land . . . that I expect will readily sell."—Tiffin to Meigs, October 4, 1817, Carter, *op. cit.*, X, 706.

[21] *Detroit Gazette*, March 13, 1818.

[22] *Ibid.*

[23] Carter, *op. cit.*, X, 740-41.

[24] *Detroit Gazette*, May 1, 1818.

[25] *Ibid.*, July 24, 1818. The lands were first offered at public auction, but those remaining unsold at the conclusion of the sale could be purchased thereafter for the minimum sale price of two dollars per acre.—Donaldson, *op. cit.*, p. 204. See also William Darby, *A Tour from the City of New York, to Detroit, in the Michigan Territory Made Between the 2nd of May and the 22nd of September, 1818* (New York, 1819), p. 200.

[26] *Detroit Gazette*, August 16, 1817; May 29, July 3, 24, 1818.

[27] *Ibid.*, September 1, 1820.

[28] *Ibid.*; A. N. Bliss, "Federal Land Grants for Internal Improvements," *Michigan*

Pioneer and Historical Society, Collections (40 vols.; Lansing, 1877-1929), VII, 52. (Hereafter cited as *M. P. H. S., C.*)

[29] *Detroit Gazette*, September 23, 1818. George N. Fuller, *Economic and Social Beginnings of Michigan. A Study of the Settlement of the Lower Peninsula During the Territorial Period, 1805-1837* (Lansing, 1916), pp. 200-01.

[30] *Ibid.*; *Detroit Gazette*, October 30, November 13, 1818.

[31] Elkanah Watson, *Men and Times of the Revolution, or Memoirs of Elkanah Watson, Including Journals of Travels in Europe and America . . .* ,Winslow C. Watson, ed. (New York, 1856), p. 429.

[32] *Detroit Gazette*, December 4, 1818.

[33] Watson, *op. cit.*, p. 430. See also Williams to Gilbert & J. B. Stuart, May 16, 1818, " John R. Williams Letterbook, 1815-1825 " (MS, in the possession of Frederick Douglas, Denver, Colorado).

[34] *Detroit Gazette*, October 16, 1818.

[35] Lewis Cass, Henry R. Schoolcraft, Henry Whiting, and John Biddle, *Historical and Scientific Sketches of Michigan, Comprising a Series of Discourses Delivered Before the Historical Society of Michigan, and Other Interesting Papers Relative to the Territory* (Detroit, 1834), pp. 163-64.

[36] *Detroit Gazette*, August 14, 1818, and July 30, 1819; Estwick Evans, " Evans' Pedestrious Tour of Four Thousand Miles—1818," in Reuben Gold Thwaites, *Early Western Travels, 1748-1846 . . .* (32 vols.; Cleveland, 1904), VIII, 219-20.

[37] *Detroit Gazette*, August 14, 1818.

[38] Almon Ernest Parkins, *The Historical Geography of Detroit* (Lansing, 1918), p. 142; Silas Farmer, *The History of Detroit and Michigan; or, the Metropolis Illustrated; A Chronological Cyclopaedia of the Past and Present . . .* (Detroit, 1884), pp. 48, 52.

[39] *Detroit Gazette*, November 21, 1817, January 2, and April 3, 1818.

[40] Farmer, *op. cit.*, p. 671.

[41] In 1820 there were only 118 subscribers in Michigan, 2 in Canada, and 32 in the rest of the United States.—*Detroit Gazette*, July 14, 1820.

[42] *Ibid.*, January 11, 1822; see also September 3, 1819, and October 5, 1821.

[43] Evans, *op. cit.*, pp. 219-22.

[44] Darby, *op. cit.*, p. 200.

[45] Watson, *op. cit.*, p. 430.

[46] Darby, *op. cit.*, p. 200.

[47] *Detroit Gazette*, May 8, 1818. Williams to Rufus Brown, May 16, 1818, " Williams Letterbook." " I now enclose herein $100 on acct. of the charges of advertising the sale of public lands in this territory. I have not yet collected any part of the subscription, but as soon as they are apportioned and received I shall lose no time in remitting you the balance."—Williams to Webster & Skinner, June 24, 1819, *ibid.*

[48] *Detroit Gazette*, October 16, 1818.

[49] *Ibid.*, December 4, 1818.

[50] The story of this company, including facsimiles of several pertinent documents relating to the purchase, is well presented in [Samuel W. Durant], *History of Oakland County . . .* (Philadelphia, 1877), pp. 68-70. See also *Detroit Gazette*, February 26, 1819.

[51] Michigan, *Laws of the Territory of Michigan* (4 vols.; Lansing, 1871-1884), II, 144-45.

[52] *Ibid.*, I, 328-29.

[53] *Detroit Gazette*, February 26, 1819.

[54] *Ibid.*, January 22, 1819.

[55] *Ibid.*, April 3, 1818.

[56] *Ibid.*, March 26, 1819. Cass held similar views.—See Cass to Calhoun, May 27, 1819, Carter, *op. cit.*, X, 827-31.

[57] *Detroit Gazette*, May 28, 1819.

[58] *Ibid.*, June 25, 1819.

[59] *Ibid.*, August 6, 1819.

[60] *Ibid.*, April 7, 1820.

[61] " Articles of a treaty made and concluded at Saginaw, in the Territory of Michigan, between the United States of America, by their Commissioner, Lewis Cass, and the Chippewa nation of Indians," September 24, 1819, *United States Statutes at Large*, VII, 203-06. Six million acres were obtained by this treaty.— *Detroit Gazette*, October 1, 1819. See also William L. Webber, " Indian Cession of 1819, Made by the Treaty of Saginaw," *M. P. H. S., C.*, XXVI, 517-34, and Ephriam S. Williams, " The Treaty of Saginaw in the Year 1819," *M. P. H. S., C.*, VII, 262-70. Brief treatments of various land cessions by the Indians and a map delineating the major cessions are in Alpheus Felch, " The Indians of Michigan and the Cession of Their Lands to the United States by Treaties," *M. P. H. S., C.*, XXVI, 274-97.

[62] *Detroit Gazette*, March 3, May 26, 1820.

[63] [Albany Argus (?)], *Outlines of the Life and Character of General Lewis Cass* (Albany, 1848), p. 24.

[64] *Detroit Gazette*, September 23, 1818; June 25, September 17, 24, 1819; and August 9, 1822.

[65] Williams to David Boyd & Co., August 1, 1818, " Williams Letterbook."

[66] Richardson, *op. cit.*, I, 647.

[67] The suspension was not applicable to that part of an individual purchase in excess of 640 acres. See " An Act further to suspend, for a limited time, the sale or forfeiture of lands, for failure in completing the payment thereon," March 30, 1820, *United States Statutes at Large*, III, 555.

[68] " An Act making further provisions for the sale of public lands," April 24, 1820, *United States Statutes at Large*, III, 566-67. See also Donaldson, *op. cit.*, p. 205.

[69] " An Act for the relief of purchasers of public lands prior to the first day of July, eighteen hundred and twenty," March 2, 1821, *United States Statutes at Large*, III, 612-14. Williams, who had speculated to some extent in real estate, declared: " The passage of that law has of course operated an entire and important change in the situation and prospects of all persons indebted to the United States for lands."—Williams to Lewis Atterberry, May 22, 1821, " Williams Letterbook."

[70] *Detroit Gazette*, August 9, 1822. At the Detroit Land Office 2,860 acres were sold in 1820, 7,444 acres in 1821, and 20,068 in 1822.—Julius P. Bolivar MacCabe, *Directory of the City of Detroit with Its Environs and Register of Michigan for the Year 1837* (Detroit, 1837), p. 86.

[71] *Detroit Gazette*, August 3, October 5, 12, 1821. In all probability " Sciawassa " is a variant of " Shiawassee," the name of a river in Michigan flowing into the Saginaw.

[72] *Ibid.*, November 2, 9, 16, 23, 1821.

96   EVERY HOUSE A FRONTIER

[73] *The Utica Sentinel*, July 2, 1822, was impressed by the possibilities of lands in the Saginaw region. Quoted in the *Detroit Gazette*, August 2, 1822.

[74] *Detroit Gazette*, June 7, 1822.

[75] " Articles of a treaty made and concluded at Chicago, in the state of Illinois, between Lewis Cass and Solomon Sibley, Commissioners of the United States, and the Ottawa, Chippewa, and Pottawatamie nation of Indians," August 29, 1821, *United States Statutes at Large*, VII, 218-221. Schoolcraft, who was secretary of the commission, described the treaty negotiations in his *Travels in the Central Portions of the Mississippi Valley*, . . . (New York, 1825), pp. 337-73. See also Bessie Louise Pierce, *A History of Chicago* (2 vols.; New York, 1937-1940), I, 29.

[76] Williams to Boyd & Suydam, September 21, 1821, " Williams Letterbook."

[77] *American State Papers, Public Lands*, III, 533; Cass, Schoolcraft, Whiting, and Biddle, *op. cit.*, p. 165.

[78] Henry R. Schoolcraft, *Narrative Journal of Travels . . . from Detroit through the Great Chain of American Lakes to the Sources of the Mississippi River . . . in the Year 1820* (Albany, 1821), p. 65. See also *Detroit Gazette*, August 10, 1821.

[79] A table consolidating data taken from publications of the state of Michigan regarding the establishment and organization of counties in southern Michigan can be found in Fuller, *op. cit.*, pp. 531-34. See also *Detroit Gazette*, January 23, 1818, March 28, 1820, and September 13, 1822.

[80] *Detroit Gazette*, September 13, 1822.

[81] *Ibid.*, February 2, 1821.

[82] *Niles' Weekly Register*, September 15, 1821.

[83] *Detroit Gazette*, May 10, 1822.

[84] *Ibid.*, June 7, 1822.

[85] *Ibid.*, June 7, October 4, 1822, and July 18, 1823.

[86] *Ibid.*, July 5, 1822. The town of Monroe was laid out in 1817 on the River Raisin, and its citizens energetically promoted the exploration and sales of lands in that region.—*Ibid.*, August 27, 1818, and June 28, 1822. Also, Fuller, *op. cit.*, p. 153.

[87] Receipts for October amounted $5,836.37.—*Detroit Gazette*, November 8, 1822.

[88] *Ibid.*, February 28, 1823.

[89] As early as 1817 Birkbeck wrote: " Land is rising rapidly in price, in all well-settled neighborhoods. Fifty dollars per acre for improved land is spoken of familiarly: I have been asked thirty for a large tract without improvements, on the Great Miami, fifty miles from Cincinnati, and similar prices in other quarters. . . . Many offers occur, all at a very great advance of price. It has now become a question, whether to fix in this comparatively populous state of Ohio or join the vast tide of emigration that is flowing farther west, where we may obtain lands of equal value at the government price of two dollars per acre. . . ."—Birkbeck, *op. cit.*, pp. 71-72. See Turner, *op. cit.*, p. 306.

[90] Quoted in the *Detroit Gazette*, March 21, 1823.

[91] *Ibid.*, May 2, 1823.

[92] Quoted in *Ibid.*, May 23, 1823.

[93] *Ibid.*, June 13, 1823.

[94] Of the thirty-eight land offices in the United States in 1821 there were only three whose receipts exceeded those of the Detroit office for the quarter ending June 30, 1821.—*Ibid.*, January 30, 1824.

[95] " An Act to establish an additional land office in the territory of Michigan," March 3, 1823, *United States Statutes at Large*, III, 778-79.

[96] *Detroit Gazette*, July 18, 1823.

[97] *Ibid.*, May 2, 1823.

[98] *Ibid.*, December 19, 1823.

[99] *Ibid.*, February 21, March 26, 1824.

[100] *Ibid.*, June 4, 1824; Fuller, *op. cit.*, p. 187.

[101] *Detroit Gazette*, July 30, 1824.

[102] Fuller, *op. cit.*, pp. 154, 172-73, 203-04; *Detroit Gazette*, October 17, 1823.

[103] *Detroit Gazette*, June 19, 26, 1818; Fuller, *op. cit.*, pp. 157-58, 161.

[104] Fuller, *op. cit.*, pp. 159-60, 164-65.

[105] *Detroit Gazette*, March 6, 26, 1824.

[106] *Ibid.*, February 28, 1824. A map portraying southeastern Michigan in 1825 is in Fuller, *op. cit.*, facing p. 632. An original copy is in the office of the Historical Commission at Lansing. This map shows the various townships referred to in the proclamations appearing in the *Gazette* at various times.

[107] The surveys were discontinued because of a cut in the federal appropriation for surveying the public lands.—*Detroit Gazette*, May 28, 1824.

[108] Acreage sold, 4,727; receipts, $5,908.60.—*Ibid.*, May 21, 1824.

[109] At the Detroit office, acreage sold 64,919.15; receipts, $77,770.69. At the Monroe office, acreage sold, 16,250.13; receipts, $20,312.66.—*Ibid.*, January 7, 14, 1825.

[110] *Ibid.*, May 21, 1824.

[111] *Ibid.*, December 24, 1824.

[112] Schoolcraft, *Travels in the Central Portions of the Mississippi Valley*, p. 6.

[113] Many others continued to arrive by sailing vessel.—*Detroit Gazette*, April 26, May 10, 24, 31, 1825.

[114] *Ibid.*, May 10, 1825.

[115] *Ibid.*, May 24, 1825.

[116] *Ibid.*, June 28, 1825.

[117] " An Act to authorize the surveying and opening of a road from Detroit to Chicago, in the state of Illinois," March 3, 1825, *United States Statutes at Large*, IV, 135. See also *Detroit Gazette*, July 26, 1825.

[118] *Detroit Gazette*, May 31, 1825.

[119] *Ibid.*, August 30, 1825; Fuller, *op. cit.*, p. 263.

[120] *Detroit Gazette*, September 20, 1825.

[121] *Ibid.*, November 15, 1825.

[122] *Ibid.*, December 13, 1825; *Michigan Herald*, April 26, 1826.

[123] In the two weeks following the arrival of the first vessel from Buffalo in the spring of 1826 more than a thousand persons landed in Detroit.—*Detroit Gazette*, May 23, 1826.

[124] Fuller, *op. cit.*, p. 132.

[125] *Detroit Gazette*, January 29, 1819 and January 2, 1824.

[126] Fuller, *op. cit.*, p. 186. In the spring of 1826 McKenney estimated the population of the city at 2,500. He probably included the settled area outside the bounds of the city.—Thomas L. McKenney, *Sketches of a Tour to the Lakes,*

of the Character and Customs of the Chippeway Indians, and of Incidents Con-
nected with the Treaty of Fond du Lac (Baltimore, 1827), p. 141.

[127] Parkins, *op. cit.*, pp. 154-58. See also *Detroit Gazette*, February 18, 1825.

[128] *Detroit Gazette*, February 18, 1825; Parkins, *op. cit.*, pp. 158-59; Fuller, *op. cit.*, p. 177.

[129] *Detroit Gazette*, February 18, 1825.

[130] H. M. Utley, " Plymouth," *M. P. H. S., C.*, I, 444-46; D. Clarkson, " Pioneer Sketches," *M. P. H. S., C.*, I, 509; Melvin D. Osband, " My Recollections of Pioneers and Pioneer Life in Nankin," *M. P. H. S., C.*, XIV, 432-33; Fuller, *op. cit.*, p. 178.

[131] Farmer, *op. cit.*, p. 25-27, 40-41.

[132] Meigs to the Governor and Judges of Michigan Territory, December 26, 1815, Meigs to Tiffin, December 26, 1815, Cass to Tiffin, January 26, 1816, Cass to Meigs, May 11, 1816, John Gardiner to Tiffin, June 6, 1816, Carter, *op. cit.*, X, 612-13, 613, 618-19, 633-35, 647. See also Farmer, *op. cit.*, p. 26.

[133] Paper entitled " Valuable Land in the Vicinity of the City of Detroit, for Sale at Public Auction, on the 16th day of September, 1816," dated June 6, 1816, " John R. Williams Papers " (MS, B. H. C.).

[134] Farmer, *op. cit.*, p. 25.

[135] *Detroit Gazette*, June 19, 1818.

[136] *Ibid.*, October 3, 1823; Farmer, *op. cit.*, p. 30.

[137] *Detroit Gazette*, October 3, 17, 1823.

[138] *Ibid.*, October 17, November 7, 1823.

[139] *Ibid.*, July 25, 1817.

[140] *Ibid.*, June 20, 1823.

[141] *Ibid.*, January 2, 1824.

[142] *Ibid.*, February 21, November 19, 1824.

[143] Farmer, *op. cit.*, p. 36.

[144] On the last day of 1825 Mayor John R. Williams wrote to Cass in Washington: " Would it be of any use if our corporation should memorialize Congress on the subject of the military ground within this city in the event of its being abandoned by the U. S. from its present purpose? "—Williams to Cass, December 31, 1825, " William Papers."

[145] Farmer, *op. cit.*, p. 36.

[146] *Ibid.*, pp. 22-23.

CHAPTER IV

Currency and Exchange

Of the numerous difficulties besetting Detroit at the conclusion of the War of 1812, none was more distressing to the public at large than the continued scarcity of valid currency. The finances of the nation were in a wretched condition. The liquidation of the Bank of the United States in 1811 had placed the burden of financing the war upon the facilities of the various state banks. These institutions issued such large amounts of inflated currency—once the control exercised by the Bank of the United States was eliminated—that they were forced to suspend payment in specie in 1814. As a consequence their notes depreciated in value, and both foreign and domestic coin disappeared from circulation. A universal demand for a remedy to correct the financial evils led to the establishment of the Second Bank of the United States in the spring of 1816. As this bank guaranteed redemption of its notes in specie, the state banks were forced to do likewise.[1] The Second Bank did not begin business until January, 1817, but in the meantime the state banks were making vigorous efforts to prepare for the resumption of specie payment.[2] They stopped discounting altogether and demanded payment from their debtors.

With this curtailment in credit, money became exceedingly scarce. In fact, nothing was in circulation in Ohio but the notes of private banks of questionable solvency.[3] The prices of land and agricultural products, as a result, had fallen to one-third the value they commanded when the excessive indebtedness was incurred during the inflationary years. Many of the 246 state banks in existence in 1816 were forced to liquidate, and many others were enabled to resume specie payments only through the assistance tendered them by the Bank of the United States.[4]

Although they continued in business, some of the western banks were on a precarious footing—concealing the true nature of their specie backing by circulating their notes over a wide area in order to limit the number that could be presented for redemption at one time. Cognizance of this situation resulted in discrimination against practically all western currency in the eastern financial centers. The paper money system had " gone beyond all bounds throughout the western country," one English traveler discovered, and " specie of the smallest amount" was rarely to be seen. Normally, the notes of reputable banks were discounted from 5 to 7½ per cent when they circulated some distance from their source. The notes of questionable banks, moreover, were discounted from 10 to 40 per cent. Specie commanded a premium of 25 per cent.[5]

Because of the peculiarities of its situation, the currency problem in Detroit was probably more acute than in any other western city. The disruption of the fur trade during the war left the city without an export staple to balance the importation of essential foods and manufactured goods. The situation was further aggravated by the exodus of capital from the city during the war years. Consequently, much of the money that entered the city left it immediately to pay for the imports.[6] To meet the money shortage in local transactions the merchants depended upon barter or upon individual due bills, which they issued in ever-increasing numbers.

Originally, due bills were issued to relieve the scarcity of silver change.[7] A merchant, on receiving a bank bill from a customer and having no fractional currency on hand to use as change, would tender notes of his own making which he promised to redeem on presentation. A farmer might barter his produce for the merchandise he needed at the moment, and accept due bills for whatever surplus remained in his favor. These he could circulate in payment of other goods and services. The practice became so widespread that mechanics, innkeepers, hucksters, clergymen, and public officials, in addition to the merchants, were issuing their own notes. Judge Woodward apparently had some of his in circulation for sums as small as one or two cents.[8] By 1817 the city was flooded with the substitute currency. In a denunciation of the practice a contributor to the *Gazette* wrote: " The issuing of small bills has of late grown so fashionable that even strangers are willing to lend us their assistance and furnish funds for our necessities the moment they arrive among us." The writer admitted that the due bills were necessary in view of the deficiency of silver currency, but he felt that they " never ought to be suffered to become the MONEY of the country." He suggested that a responsible company be formed to issue small bills in order that they would come from one source and not from a hundred.[9] The uncertainty of redemption depreciated them to such an extent that they circulated at but two-thirds their nominal value.[10] A contemporary declared that there were some persons in Detroit who could not redeem the notes they had issued if given three months to do it. He recommended that the city follow a procedure instituted in New York, where the city corporation was the sole authorized issuer of small bills for marketing purposes. Any profit accruing would be for the public good, and the holders of the bills would be sure of their redemption. Not until such a measure was adopted, he felt, would silver be seen in general circulation.[11] No action was taken however, and the practice continued.

By 1819 irregularities in the procedure had become so serious that a citizens' committee met and adopted the following resolutions:

Resolved, that the issuing of small change notes, by individuals who do not redeem them at sight, is an evil which
we pledge ourselves to endeavor to correct.

Resolved, that any person issuing small bills after the
first day of March next shall give security to the public for
the faithful and punctual redemption of said bills.

Resolved, as the sense of this meeting, that we will not
circulate or give currency to the bills of any individual after
the first day of March next, who shall fail to redeem them
within three days from their presentation for payment.[12]

One of the signers deemed it prudent to redeem his notes immediately " as well to make room for other *unchartered* bankers, as
to relieve persons in the retail trade from a portion of the embar-
rassment occasioned by a surplus of this depreciated medium." [13]
Gabriel Richard signified his willingness to take his small notes
in payment for a plot of land he had for sale.[14] The prevalence
of counterfeit change notes in the city served to intensify public
resentment.[15]

As specie gradually returned, the need for a substitute currency
diminished. This continued in circulation, however, until late in
1822, when a group of ninety-seven influential citizens pledged
that they would no longer pass individual due bills nor receive
them in trade.[16] This action was effective in ending their existence.

With the return of silver, " cut " money once again made its
appearance, and by 1820 there was so much in circulation that
it constituted a " grievous nuisance." The *Gazette* condemned the
practice of cutting money as " a species of fraud exercised by
some despicable person or persons . . ." and added: " There is
scarcely a day passes but numerous bits of silver are offered to
our traders, some of which are a third and many a quarter less
than their nominal value." [17] It urged all citizens to refuse " cut "
money except by weight. This would put an end to the " nefarious
practice " and prevent any further mutilation of the currency.
" For ourselves," stated the editor, " we can only promise that

when we correctly ascertain who these money-cutting swindlers are, they shall be noticed in so conspicuous a manner that, however innocent they may deem the practice, every child in the street shall be acquainted with their occupation." [18] Despite this strong condemnation almost a year passed before there was any concerted action to outlaw "cut" money. In August, 1821, "at a very numerous meeting of the citizens of Detroit," a resolution was adopted whereby cut coin was refused currency. The signers pledged themselves to do everything in their power to discontinue its circulation.[19] This action was effective in putting an end to money-cutting in the city, and thereafter the pieces were sold by the ounce and converted into ornaments for the Indian trade.[20]

Another form of substitute money current in Detroit at this time was scrip. That first issued by the Governor and Judges in 1819 was in bills of two, three, five, ten, and twenty dollars. It bore interest at the rate of 6 per cent and was to be redeemed out of the proceeds of the sale of lands in the Ten Thousand Acre Tract, but the lands had sold at such a low price that it depreciated in value. As early as 1820 it passed at a discount of 10 per cent. By 1826, $22,500 in scrip of this type had been issued.[21]

Wayne County was in severe financial straits at this time. The tax levy in 1819 and 1820 was largely uncollected, and to meet the deficiency in receipts the county commissioners issued scrip which was to be redeemed out of future collections. No tax was levied in 1821, however, and by March, 1822 the county was about three thousand dollars in debt.[22] Consequently, the scrip depreciated to such an extent that it passed at a discount of 25 per cent.[23]

Most of the bank bills that circulated in Detroit were from Ohio institutions; some were from Pennsylvania and Kentucky. Not until the Bank of Michigan began business in 1819 were there notes circulating that could be redeemed locally. In the meantime the city was forced to depend upon a variety of currency to pay for its imports. Even many of the federal disbursements—

which were so vital to the welfare of the city—were made in Ohio bank paper.[24] During 1817, however, the bills of the chartered banks passed freely at a small discount in the city, but those of the unchartered banks were accepted at a higher rate of discount.[25] The fact that they passed so readily was probably due to the great need of facilities to reimburse Ohio exporters of meat and flour.

The resumption of specie payments in 1817—dictated by federal legislation—caused a precipitate depreciation in the value of notes issued by the unchartered banks, for the majority of them were deficient in specie backing. By the end of the year most of the unchartered banks in Ohio had failed, leaving thousands of worthless notes in the hands of individuals throughout the West.[26]

Matters took a more serious turn, however, when the chartered banks began "to shake."[27] The return to par of a currency depreciated on the average 25 per cent produced a sudden fall in prices, but debts contracted in the depreciated currency remained at the same nominal amount. When the banks once again curtailed credit in an endeavor to maintain specie payments, they found it difficult to make collections.[28] An uncertainty developed in regard to the ability of many to redeem in specie, and, as a result, their issues began to decline in value. The growing anxiety of Detroit citizens concerning Ohio currency was evidenced by an editorial in the *Gazette* in which recommendations were made that banks be limited in number and their backing secured by legislative means. In addition to the private institutions there were nearly fifty chartered banks in Pennsylvania and thirty in Ohio. According to the *Gazette*:

> New ones are continually rising or endeavoring to rise, with or without capital, as the case may be. Others, which have for a time maintained an extensive credit, are failing and, from inability or disinclination, refuse to redeem their bills. Notes are often found in circulation on banks, which have a " name " indeed, but no " local habitation." A great

part of the community are unable to detect these frauds, and the loss which is sustained by them must be immense.[29]

Merchants depended upon the publication of bank-note exchanges for information regarding the financial status of the banks, but by the middle of 1818 the picture changed so rapidly that the quotations were obsolete before they reached the city.[30] The uncertainty was heightened by the spread of rumors unfavorable to institutions with good reputations. The *Gazette* believed that many of the rumors originated with speculators interested in purchasing bills at a high rate of discount in Detroit and exchanging them at a profit at their place of issue.[31]

Soon the distress was nation-wide. Specie left the country in large amounts in consequence of the premiums offered by English exporters who held huge balances against American merchants.[32] American manufacturing industries, inflated by the Embargo Act and the war, were ruined by the importation of large amounts of cheaper foreign merchandise, and many laborers were thrown out of employment.[33] Even the Bank of the United States was in such desperate straits that it was forced to curtail credit. On extremely short notice it called upon its debtor banks for payment in specie.[34] Even though the Ohio banks had greatly reduced their note issues, this action forced most of them to suspend specie payments.[35] It was estimated that $800,000 in specie was drawn from Ohio in the twelve-month period ending in June, 1819; and, according to one authority, " the wonder is not that only six or seven banks in that state paid specie in August, 1819, but that they were not all bankrupt." [36]

Meanwhile, in Detroit, the decline in currency value gave rise to a situation bordering on the chaotic. The *Gazette* begged those possessing " competent knowledge " to volunteer information concerning various Ohio banks.[37] Shortly thereafter, for the benefit of its readers, it classified the banks as " good," " decent," " middling," and " good for nothing." [38] At a citizens' meeting early in December, 1819, a committee was appointed to draft resolutions for " the diffusion of intelligence relative to the value of the money in circulation in this territory, and the state of those Ohio and other banks which have sent their notes to be circulated in it." [39] The committee investigated the paying ability of the Ohio banks, and, a week later, submitted the following resolutions:

> Resolved, that we consider those banks which do not redeem their notes with specie as unworthy of confidence and that we will use all laudable means to prevent the introduction and circulation of their notes in this territory.

> Resolved, that a committee of five citizens be appointed, whose duty it shall be to make diligent inquiry into the state of those banks that have notes in circulation in this territory, and that they publish weekly the results of their inquiries in the *Detroit Gazette* in some plain and concise manner.

The resolutions were adopted and a committee was appointed to conduct the investigations for a period of three months, after which a new one was to be appointed. In accordance with its instructions the committee decided that the notes of all banks maintaining specie payment would be accepted at par in the territory, while all those of institutions which refused to redeem in specie would be subject to a discount of 20 per cent. It compiled a list of banks whose notes ought to circulate on these terms; those not listed were felt to be " of such doubtful character, as to render it impossible for the committee to determine the value of their notes." [40]

This action was effective in curbing the circulation of the distrusted currency. Merchants expressed their determination to accept no other notes but those recommended by the committee— and then only on the terms it suggested.[41] People were so anxious to get rid of depreciated Ohio currency that the editor of the *Gazette* felt that they might be accused of extravagance. The notes gradually disappeared, however, and he expressed the belief that " in a few weeks longer they will have all departed ' like the

baseless fabric of a vision,' " but he dared not hope that they would
" ' leave not a *wreck* behind.' " [42]

The counterfeiting of bank notes added to the financial confusion. The *Niles' Weekly Register* noted: " Counterfeiting goes
on prosperously, and presents itself in so many forms that it is
difficult to guard against it." It added: " We can hardly take up
a newspaper without seeing some fresh evidence of the prostra-
tion of morals caused by the paper system." [43] Under the heading
" Caution Necessary," the *Gazette* published a list of spurious
bills circulating in the western country. [44] The cashier of the Bank
of Michigan warned that " some knave " had commenced altering
its notes, and offered a reward for the apprehension of those
engaged in the " nefarious business." [45]

Although the depreciation of the Ohio bank paper had caused
much suffering in Detroit, [46] its plight was alleviated somewhat by
the establishment of the Bank of Michigan, which was authorized
by the Territorial Legislature and incorporated in June, 1818.
Its capital was limited to $100,000. The stock was placed on
the market at the time of incorporation, the shares selling at
$100 each, ten dollars of which was demanded in specie at the time
of purchase. No bills were to be issued until $10,000 in specie
had been accumulated, and further installments were to be paid
at the discretion of the directors. [47]

Detroit welcomed the new bank. " We heartily congratulate the
citizens of Michigan on the prospect of this institution soon being
able to relieve them from the trash of Ohio, which has so long
impoverished the country by its uncertain value," wrote the editor
of the *Gazette*. " The interests of commerce," he added, " must
also feel the beneficial effects of a bank, which goes into operation
with every appearance of a solid, durable, and responsible character." [48] When the first bills were issued in the early part of
January, 1819, there was $12,000 in specie to back them. [49] The
Gazette, nevertheless, expressed the hope that the directors would
" act openly and fairly, and *profit by the thousand warning pre-*

cedents which they have before them, as well as their own experience." [50]

The bank was conducted in a conservative manner and soon won public confidence. It arrived on the scene at a time when trustworthy currency was hardly obtainable. Several years later John R. Williams, its first president, commented upon the effects produced by its establishment:

> Our territory then inundated with depreciated currency, the stamp of uncertainty and loss was fixed upon every commercial transaction until some time after the establishment of the Bank of Michigan, when the introduction of a currency founded on a solid basis caused all the miserable and depreciated trash soon to disappear.[51]

The territory proved to be a ripe field for banking operations, and at the end of the first year the bank appeared to be safely launched on a prosperous career. Williams declared at that time: " Thus far the business of the institution has been so conducted that not a single dollar has been lost or jeopardized by bad debts." [52] As an indication of its soundness the Secretary of the Treasury directed the Receiver of Public Moneys in Detroit to accept its bills.[53] Pursuant to law, the bank submitted a report of its condition to the Governor and Judges, which proved to be highly satisfactory.[54] In January, 1822 it declared a dividend for the last six months of 1821 of 4 per cent on the paid-in capital. A dividend of 6 per cent on paid-in capital followed for 1822, and 7 per cent for 1823.[55] At no time during these years was there any doubt of the bank's ability to redeem its notes with specie —in fact, there was probably never a time that its circulation exceeded its specie backing.[56]

While the conservative policy maintained by the management assured the integrity of the bank, it was incompatible with the growing commercial activity of the area. With its limited capital the bank was unable to satisfy the rising demand for credit.

Williams, as president, opposed an expansion of its facilities for fear that control of the institution would pass from the hands of Detroit citizens.[57] His banking philosophy was expressed in a letter to an eastern associate:

> Our situation is different in this country from yours. We have no monied institutions or private sources from which money can be obtained on good security. We have indeed a bank but its capital being small and the wants of the community very great and general it became necessary to accommodate generally so as to render the institution as it ought to be—a public benefit instead of a convenience for a few individuals. Thus far it has been properly conducted and I trust it will continue so to be. I would rather submit to any inconvenience than to yield to any measure that would be likely to affect its reputation.[58]

In 1823, five years after its stock was first offered for sale, only $15,000 of the authorized $100,000 capital had been acquired. Even the cautious Williams admitted that an increase in the active capital would be to the advantage of the stockholders.[59] Much to his dismay, however, Henry Dwight, a financier of Geneva, New York, succeeded in obtaining two hundred shares of the stock. This transfer of stock placed control of the bank in the hands of Dwight and other eastern stockholders.[60] Immediately thereafter, in order to increase the working capital, the board of directors demanded the payment of a second installment of ten dollars on each share of the stock.[61] Within a short time the paid-in capital was increased to $60,000.[62] Williams was not in agreement with the policies pursued by Dwight and his associates, and since he believed that monopolies were injurious to a community, he resigned the presidency.[63] Some months later, in a letter to Dwight, he pointed out that the rapid development of the territory would assure the bank a prosperous future, but he warned that it would be " dangerous to force matters beyond the

speed which the growing state of the country and other circumstances" would justify.[64]

Despite his fears, the bank was blessed with good management,
and its increase in capital enabled it to render excellent service
to the commercial interests of the expanding city.[65] In the spring
of 1825, shortly after Eurotus P. Hastings became president, it
was discovered that the cashier had been appropriating funds for
his own use over a period of years. The defalcation constituted
a large proportion of the paid-in capital, but the capitalists con-
trolling the bank had sufficient resources to cushion the loss—and
its reputation remained unimpaired.[66]

In addition to providing the city with a sound currency, the
Bank of Michigan furnished Detroit merchants with facilities for
reimbursing eastern creditors. During the years immediately following the war, local merchants continued having great difficulty
in securing exchange acceptable in the East. It was necessary to
forward money to the seaboard in consequence of a trade balance
highly unfavorable to Detroit.[67] As late as 1821 furs were about
the only export product which could be profitably transported
to the East, but they could not be gathered in sufficient quantity
to compensate for the imports.[68]

While western bank money was satisfactory to Ohio creditors,
it continued to be discounted so drastically in New York that a
Detroiter could ill-afford to use it in payment of his eastern debts.[69]
Currency acceptable at par or at nominal discount in the East
was difficult to obtain. The few newcomers to Detroit and the
occasional visitor brought with them eastern bank bills and United
States Treasury notes which the merchants hoarded in order to
meet eastern obligations.[70] Late in 1816 this situation was relieved
somewhat by the decision of the War Department to pay the
troops stationed at Detroit in eastern currency.[71] Various types of
credit instruments redeemable in the East in eastern currency or in
specie were much sought after in order to satisfy the remaining
balances. Much of this credit was made available by the disburse-

ments of the federal government for the support of the military forces in the territory and for the maintenance of the Indian Department.[72]

In Detroit, United States officials paid for supplies with drafts or bills of exchange which were redeemable in the East out of federal funds. Williams sometimes obtained drafts issued by the army quartermaster at Detroit on the Quartermaster-General in New York and used them to pay his eastern creditors.[73] At other times he paid with bills of exchange issued by army officers or the army contractor.[74] Now and then he secured bills of exchange from private sources,[75] and once he was " so fortunate as to obtain a check on the cashier of the Mechanic's Bank, New York, for one thousand dollars. . . ." [76]

During these years, however, there was seldom sufficient eastern exchange to satisfy the needs of Detroit merchants. Consequently, credit instruments redeemable in eastern currency frequently commanded a premium.[77] Even so, at times merchants found it impossible to secure eastern exchange in any form. Government expenditures diminished with the reduction of the military forces in Detroit—thus decreasing exchange facilities. In 1818 payments for land served to remove much of the circulating medium from the city and further reduced the exchange available.[78] The growing uncertainty regarding the value of western money engendered a reluctance among the holders of negotiable eastern paper to accept anything in exchange but currency of equal worth. By January, 1818, Williams was experiencing great difficulty in procuring exchange, and in July he wrote to an eastern creditor that although he had a thousand dollars on hand in western money, his inability to purchase a draft on the East prevented his remitting it.[79]

The necessity of utilizing exchange in whatever form he could secure it caused the Detroit merchant a great amount of inconvenience. Seldom could he pay the exact amount due an eastern creditor. Small drafts could be forwarded and credited to his account at one establishment, but if he managed to secure a draft for a large amount, he might wish to divide it among several creditors. If so, he would send it to one of them with instructions as to how it should be apportioned. Sometimes he would deposit the draft with one house and then draw on it for whatever remained in his favor with bills of exchange, which he forwarded to other creditors.[80]

Soon after its establishment the Bank of Michigan became the clearing-house for eastern exchange. Holders of credit instruments on New York and other seaboard cities were not averse to the acceptance of its bills since they were redeemable in specie at all times.[81] Subsequently, the bank forwarded the drafts to New York and deposited them in banks in that city. Thereafter, when a Detroit merchant had occasion to make payment on an eastern account, he would purchase a draft at the Bank of Michigan on an eastern institution and forward it to his creditor.[82] At times, during the early 'twenties, the bank found it impossible to sell eastern drafts due to the exhaustion of its credit in New York. These periods were of brief duration, however, and were determined by the time involved in transporting credit instruments to the East and in communicating the acknowledgement of deposit to Detroit.[83] With the increase in population in the territory and the resultant growth in its trade and commerce, eastern exchange became more abundant in Detroit; and with the expansion of its facilities, the Bank of Michigan eliminated most of the difficulties formerly experienced in making eastern remittances.

Several years elapsed before the bills of the Bank of Michigan found ready acceptance outside of the territory. They were first issued at a time when almost all western money was in high disfavor. In the East there remained memories of the short-lived Bank of Detroit and the losses sustained when it failed to redeem the thousands of notes it placed in circulation.[84] As late as 1825 Boston merchants were attempting to curb the passage of the bills of the Bank of Michigan, intimating that the public could once again be defrauded.[85] Within a year after their issuance, however, the bills were accepted in payment of debts as far away as Chilli-cothe.[86] By 1823 the conservative policy pursued by the manage-ment of the bank earned an even wider acceptance for its bills. Williams wrote to a creditor at Buffalo: "I presume that our bills will pass current at your place, as an arrangement on terms of mutual reciprocity has been entered into between the Bank of Michigan and that of Geneva." [87] Late in 1824 the *Gazette* pointed out that as an illustration of the confidence which people had in the solvency and stability of the bank, a New York broker had offered to redeem its bills at one per cent discount.[88] Within a short time New York merchants were accepting the bills at the same rate, thus providing a ready medium for settling eastern accounts. In November, 1825 an Albany merchant wrote to Williams: " We perceive the Michigan Bank bills are redeemed at small disct. in N. Y.—these will no doubt answer us very well if more convenient to you." [89] By the next spring they were con-sidered as good as the bills of the banks of western New York and of other eastern states, and New York merchants received them at par on all their accounts.[90]

CHAPTER IV—NOTES

[1] Davis Rich Dewey, *Financial History of the United States* (12th ed.; New York, London, Toronto, 1934), pp. 144-50; Elmer H. Youngman, " Banking in the United States," and William A. Scott, " The Monetary System of the United States," *Encyclopedia Americana* (30 vols.; New York, 1941), III, 171-73; XIX, 349.

[2] A joint resolution of Congress at the time the Second Bank was authorized provided that after February 20, 1817 all dues to the federal government must be paid in legal currency, treasury notes, the notes of the Bank of the United States, or the notes of those state banks which redeemed their issues in United States currency. Thus the state banks were given about ten months to make the necessary arrangements for redemption in specie. Otherwise they would have no financial standing with the federal government, nor could they expect to do business with the Bank of the United States.—Dewey, *op. cit.*, p. 151. See also Youngman, *op. cit.*, p. 172.

[3] Dudley Woodbridge to William Woodbridge, October 16, 1818, " William Woodbridge Papers " (MS, Burton Historical Collection, Detroit Public Library; hereafter cited as B. H. C.).

[4] Youngman, *op. cit.*, p. 172; Dewey, *op. cit.*, p. 144.

[5] Henry Bradshaw Fearon, *Sketches of America. A Narrative of a Journey of*

Five Thousand Miles through the Eastern and Western States of America (3rd ed.; London, 1819), pp. 232-33; *Detroit Gazette*, August 8, 1817.

[6] Williams to Boyd & Suydam, September 23, 1815, John R. Williams, " Letter-book, 1815-1825 " (MS in the possession of Frederick Douglas, Denver, Colorado).

[7] " It is believed than on an average, there is not a copper coin in the possession of more than one individual out of three hundred in this territory who are in the practice of receiving and paying money."—*Detroit Gazette*, September 17, 1819.

[8] Silas Farmer, *The History of Detroit and Michigan; or, the Metropolis Illustrated; A Chronological Cyclopedia of the Past and Present* . . . (Detroit, 1884), p. 847.

[9] *Detroit Gazette*, September 5, 12, 1817. See also Farmer, *op. cit.*, p. 847.

[10] *Detroit Gazette*, October 3, 1817.

[11] *Ibid.*, October 10, 1817.

[12] *Ibid.*, February 5, 1819.

[13] *Ibid.*

[14] *Ibid.*, May 7, 1819.

[15] *Ibid.*, June 25, 1819

[16] *Ibid.*, October 18, 1822.

[17] *Ibid.*, September 29, 1820.

[18] *Ibid.*

[19] *Ibid.*, August 24, 1821.

[20] Charles C. Trowbridge, " Detroit Past and Present in Relation to Its Social and Physical Condition," *Michigan Pioneer and Historical Society, Collections* (40 vols.; Lansing, 1877-1912, 1915-1929), I, 382. (Hereafter cited as *M. P. H. S., C.*)

[21] A facsimile of such scrip is in Farmer, *op. cit.*, p. 474. See also pp. 475, 847; Williams to Webb & Drummer, May 13, 1820, " Williams Letterbook "; and *Detroit Gazette*, November 28, 1823.

[22] *Detroit Gazette*, March 15, 1822.

[23] *Ibid.*, November 30, 1821.

[24] *Niles' Weekly Register*, January 18, 1817.

[25] *Detroit Gazette*, August 8, 1817.

[26] " The notes of our unchartered banks are now, with one or two exceptions, nearly out of circulation. When we say out of circulation, we do not mean that they have been called in and honorably redeemed. Far from it. Thousands and tens of thousands of them are scattered over the country and lie useless in the hands of their possessors, who indulge the hope that at some future period they will pass—out of their hands at some rate or other."—*Muskingum Messenger*, quoted in *ibid.*, January 2, 1818, without a date given.

[27] *Detroit Gazette*, January 2, 1818.

[28] [Richard Hildreth], *The History of Banks: to Which is Added, a Demonstration of the Advantage and Necessity of Free Competition in the Business of Banking* (Boston, 1837), p. 66.

[29] *Detroit Gazette*, April 17, 1818.

[30] Information from Grotjan's, *Philadelphia Bank Note Exchange* of May 4, 1818, was printed in *ibid.*, July 3, 1818.

[31] *Detroit Gazette*, July 3, October 9, 1818, and July 23, 1819.

[32] *Cincinnati Gazette*, quoted in *ibid.*, December 11, 1818.

[33] Dewey, *op. cit.*, pp. 152, 166.

[34] *Ibid.*, p. 152; *Cincinnati Gazette*, quoted in the *Detroit Gazette*, December 11, 1818; Hildreth, *op. cit.*, pp. 66-67; William M. Gouge, *A Short History of Paper Money and Banking in the United States, Including an Account of Provincial and Continental Paper Money* . . . (Phildelphia, 1833), Part 2, p. 129.

[35] Hildreth, *op. cit.*, p. 66; *Cincinnati Gazette*, quoted in *Detroit Gazette*, December 11, 1818.

[36] Gouge, *op. cit.*, Part 2, p. 129.

[37] *Detroit Gazette*, September 10, 1819.

[38] *Ibid.*, October 22, 1819.

[39] *Ibid.*, December 10, 1819.

[40] *Ibid.*, December 17, 1819.

[41] *Ibid.*, January 28, 1820. " Respecting information relative to the Ohio banks it is not in my power to furnish you with any better than the enclosed statement taken from the *Detroit Gazette* will afford you, with this single remark that the less you take of the descriptions of bank paper which is not redeemed with specie on demand, the better."—Williams to Capt. Jedediah Rogers, April 1, 1820, " Williams Letterbook."

[42] *Detroit Gazette*, January 28, 1820.

[43] *Niles' Weekly Register*, May 15, 1819.

[44] *Detroit Gazette*, May 21, 1819.

[45] *Ibid.*, June 4, 1819.

[46] As late as November 30, 1821, the *Gazette* remarked: " The number of our confirmed debtors is daily increasing. . . ."

[47] For the complete text of the act authorizing the establishment of the Bank of Michigan see *Laws of the Territory of Michigan* (4 vols.; Lansing, 1871-1884), I, 438-47. See also *Detroit Gazette*, May 12, 1818; Williams to David Stone, January 14, 1820, " Williams Letterbook."

[48] *Detroit Gazette*, June 12, 1818.

[49] *Ibid.*, January 8, 1819; Williams to Dwight, January 12, 1825, " Williams Letterbook "; Williams to Dwight, January 12, 1825, " John R. Williams Papers " (MS, B. H. C.).

[50] *Detroit Gazette*, January 8, 1819.

[51] Williams' letter of resignation as president of the Bank of Michigan to the board of directors, November 17, 1824, " Williams Papers."

[52] Williams felt that the bank stock was a good investment. He said: " The geographical situation of the country, its local advantages, the large disbursements of the government in this quarter—our trade—our resources and the circumstance of there being but one bank in all this extensive country—all these circumstances combine to promise a favorable and advantageous and increasingly profitable result to the stockholders."—Williams to Stone, January 14, 1820, " Williams Letterbook."

[53] *Detroit Gazette*, September 1, 1820.

[54] *Ibid.*, January 28, 1821.

[55] *Ibid.*, January 18, 1822, January 10, 1823, January 9, 1824.

[56] *Ibid.*, March 15, 1822, January 10, 1823. " We have now a certain and real medium currency—which truly represents specie—instead of the immense varieties of depreciated paper currency which was thrown into circulation from almost every quarter of the Union, occasioning great damage to the community and loss by individuals throughout the Territory."—Williams to [Stone], July 30, 1823, " Williams Papers."

[57] Williams to Stone, July 30, 1823, Williams to the directors of the Bank of Michigan, November 17, 1824, Williams to [Henry Dwight], January 12, 1825, "Williams Papers"; Williams to [Dwight], January 12, 1825, "Williams Letterbook."

[58] Williams to Boyd & Suydam, February 24, 1822, "Williams Letterbook."

[59] Stone to the president and directors of the Bank of Michigan, July 23, 1823, and Williams to Stone, July 30, 1823, "Williams Papers."

[60] Williams to the directors of the Bank of Michigan, July 10, 1824, Williams to James McCloskey, July 10, 1824, Williams to Dwight, January 12, 1825, "Williams Papers"; Williams to Dwight, January 12, 1825, "Williams Letterbook." See also Clarence M. Burton, *The City of Detroit, Michigan 1701-1922* (5 vols., Detroit, 1922), I, 627-28, 631. Other eastern stockholders are named in Farmer, *op. cit.*, p. 859.

[61] *Detroit Gazette*, August 6, 1824.

[62] Farmer, *op. cit.*, p. 859.

[63] Williams to the board of directors of the Bank of Michigan, November 17, 1824, "Williams Papers."

[64] Williams to Dwight, January 12, 1825, "Williams Letterbook."

[65] Burton, *op. cit.*, I, 631.

[66] Burton claims the loss amounted to $10,300.—*Ibid.*, I, 627. Farmer, *op. cit.*, p. 859, places it at $15,000.

[67] David Thomas, *Travels Through the Western Country in the Summer of 1816* . . . (Auburn, N. Y., 1819), p. 315.

[68] *Detroit Gazette*, June 1, 1821.

[69] In a letter to the Paymaster-General, Macomb claimed: " Such has been the distress of the officers generally on account of the depreciated currency in which they have been paid in this department that their debts to the eastward have been left totally unpaid—the exchange being 25 per cent against the western money."— Macomb to Brent, November 10, 1816, Alexander Macomb, "Letterbook, 1807-1819" (Typescript, B. H. C.). "I have about $2,500 on hand which I cannot think sending to New York, the bills being principally fives, tens, etc.; besides, the difference of exchange deters me. . . ."—Williams to Boyd & Suydam, March 15, 1817, "Williams Letterbook." See also Boyd & Suydam to Williams, May 23, 1816, "Williams Papers."

[70] Williams to Thomas H. & A. Leggett, August 21, 1817, "Williams Letterbook." Congress authorized the issuance of Treasury notes shortly after the outbreak of war in 1812. They were in reality United States scrip, bearing interest at 5⅖ per cent and redeemable out of federal receipts in one year. Some were issued in amounts as small as $3.00. They constituted a more stable currency than bank bills.—See Dewey, *op. cit.*, pp. 135-38.

[71] Macomb to Brent, November 10, 1816, "Macomb Letterbook."

[72] Thomas, *op. cit.*, p. 315

[73] "I shall settle by drafts which I contemplate sending in a few days as the Qr. Master daily expects power to draw on New York."—Williams to Boyd & Suydam, July 10, 1817, "Williams Letterbook." See also Williams to Rufus Brown, August 16, 1817, Williams to Cornell & Nostrand, January 24, 1818, "Williams Letterbook."

[74] Williams to Boyd & Suydam, May 3, 1817, Williams to Caldwell & Solomon, June 20, 1817, Williams to Starr & Smith, July 27, 1818, "Williams Letterbook."

[75] Williams to John Ray, August 21, 1817, Williams to David J. Boyd & Co., August 1, 1818, Williams to Gilbert & J. B. Stuart, October 2, 1818, " Williams Letterbook."

[76] Williams to Boyd & Suydam, November 16, 1816, " Williams Letterbook."

[77] In a letter to an eastern creditor in which he enclosed a draft for $400 Williams wrote: " I cannot consent to allow any discount on the drft. If money equivalent to New York Curr'y is not paid for it please to send it back, as I have already paid a premium for it."—Williams to John Ray, August 21, 1817, " Williams Letterbook." See also *Detroit Gazette*, April 14, 1820.

[78] Williams to David J. Boyd & Co., August 1, 1818, Williams to [Gilbert & J. B. Stuart], November 14, 1818, " Williams Letterbook."

[79] Williams to Boyd & Suydam, January 23, July 18, 1818, " Williams Letterbook."

[80] Williams to Starr & Smith, December 30, 1815, Williams to Wilbur & Fish, December 30, 1815, Williams to Henry Lote, December 30, 1815, Williams to David J. Boyd & Co., August 1, 1818, " Williams Letterbook."

[81] *Detroit Gazette*, March 15, 1822.

[82] " I enclose to you herein a Dft. on Lynde Catlin, Esq., Cashier of the U. S. Office of Disct. and Deposit of New York drawn by James McCloskey, Cashier of the Bank of Michigan, dated this day for the sum of One Hundred Dollars— which is made payable to your order. . . ."—Williams to Blecker & Sedgewick, January 8, 1820, " Williams Letterbook." Later, most of the drafts were drawn on the Branch Bank of the United States at New York.—Williams to A. Wakeman, April 14, 1821, Williams to I. & H. Meacham, December 4, 1823, Williams to John H. Webb, December 11, 1823, " Williams Letterbook."

[83] Williams wrote to an eastern creditor: " I must entreat your indulgence for a few days more for the balance of your account for transportation, etc. Our cashier has not yet returned, but is hourly expected; when he arrives we shall be in eastern funds."—Williams to John Scott, November 16, 1820, " Williams Letterbook." See also Williams to A. Wakeman, March 24, 1821, " Williams Letterbook."

[84] For an account of the Bank of Detroit, the first financial institution to be established in Michigan, see Farmer, *op. cit.*, pp. 654-58 and C. M. Burton, *op. cit.*, I, pp. 622-27.

[85] The citizens of Detroit were incensed by this action and held meetings to protest the measures adopted in Boston.—*Detroit Gazette*, February 18, 25, 1825.

[86] *Ibid.*, January 7, 1820.

[87] Williams to Townsend & Coit, September 17, 1823, " Williams Letterbook."

[88] *Detroit Gazette*, September 10, 1824. After Dwight and his associates gained control of the Bank of Michigan in 1824, they took steps to gain wider acceptance of its bills and to increase the number in circulation. Dwight, who was also president of the Bank of Geneva, New York, arranged to distribute the bills throughout the East. Funds of the Bank of Michigan were deposited in the Bank of Geneva in order to guarantee the redemption of the bills in the East. This measure was successful in raising their value to a par with eastern bank bills.— Dwight to Williams, October 6, November 20, 1824, " Williams Papers." Williams to the directors of the Bank of Michigan, July 10, 1824, Williams to McCloskey, July 10, 1824, " Williams Papers."

[89] Rufus H. King & Co. to Williams, November 25, 1825, " Williams Papers."

[90] H. H. Schieffelin & Co. to Dr. Wm. McCloskey, June 8, 1826, " Williams Papers."

CHAPTER V

Commerce and Industry

It has been pointed out that the confusion wrought in the Detroit area by the War of 1812 precluded a return to the way of life pursued by the inhabitants prior to the war and that those interested in the rehabilitation of the city recognized the need of a more diversified economy to strengthen its position and to end its dependency upon the rest of the nation. The disruption of the fur trade during the war years had deprived the city of its chief means of sustenance and had rendered destitute most of those who had depended upon it for employment. " The fatal mistake of educating a whole community for a single and temporary business is now seriously felt and acknowledged," wrote Cass at this time.[1] Cognizant of the agricultural deficiencies of the French population, and having more faith in an economy of the soil than in that of the forest, he urged the Americanization of the area as the best means of solving its problems. The Tiffin report—and its aftermath—put an end to the immediate realization of his hopes. Major-General Alexander Macomb, in command of the troops at Detroit, had similar ideas. Learning that his forces were to be employed in opening the road between Detroit and the Ohio settlements, he wrote to his superior:

We will be the means of introducing a more industrious race of people and thereby invigorate this extreme point of the national limits, and afford a more certain mode of subsisting our forces stationed on these waters.[2]

For several years, however, American migration to the territory was too small to have much effect on the community. The *habitants* seemed content with their lot, making little effort to better their status. Instead of availing themselves of the ready market for agricultural products offered by the city and the garrison, many turned once again to the uncertainties of their first love—the Indian trade.

Following the war there was a great demand for furs in eastern markets and in Europe.[3] The opportunities for great wealth to be derived from the fur trade had become proverbial.[4] Even before the conclusion of the war, Ramsay Crooks, as agent for John Jacob Astor, traveled through the western country endeavoring to purchase furs in order to profit by favorable markets.[5] In the spring of 1815 Detroit merchants spared no expense to obtain the goods necessary for a resumption of the trade and to get them to Detroit in time to secure a portion of the furs brought to the post. " Although my journey was disagreeable and fatiguing . . . I arrived here in plenty good time," wrote Williams in July. " My remittances will show you," he added, " that you may depend that I have not been idle . . . it becomes us to strike the iron while it is hot. . . ."[6] Two weeks later he wrote to the same creditor: " Business must be pretty good, to be candid I have sold more goods than ever in the same period of time. . . . Everything is in having quick supplies."[7]

Most of the furs collected by the merchants in 1815 were obtained directly from the large numbers of Indians encamped in the vicinity of the post. In the fall of 1815 traders again left the city for their winter stations, having secured their trade goods from Detroit merchants on credit. They returned with their collections in the late spring of the next year. It was customary for the traders to give to those merchants who had furnished them with trade goods the preference in purchasing their furs.[8] When news arrived in the spring of 1816 of a substantial advance in the market price of furs, great activity was displayed by the merchants in Detroit. Williams noted that the competition for furs was strong, and that his inability to purchase them on a commission basis for a New York capitalist was due to " the traders from Boston," who, he claimed, " give high prices and take all kinds, therefore obtain the preference." [9] The confidence inspired by the high market price of furs led to expanded activity in the trade, and the fall of the year found a larger corps of traders heading for the Indian country.[10]

Meanwhile, in the spring of 1816 Congress passed an act which made it illegal for a foreign organization to participate in the fur trade within the confines of the United States.[11] As early as 1808, when he organized the American Fur Company, John Jacob Astor was formulating plans for gaining a monopoly of the fur trade in American territory—even as far west as the Pacific Ocean.[12] In 1811 he succeeded in joining forces with the two major English companies operating in the United States, forming a partnership known as the South West Company.[13] During the War of 1812 he made further plans for gaining control of the trade,[14] and early in 1817, shortly after the congressional action eliminating foreign interests from the field, he bought out his partners in the South West Company—thus obtaining for the American Fur Company [15] a virtual monopoly of the trade in the United States. As early as 1816 Astor's chief agent, Ramsay Crooks, appeared in Detroit, and, after a short stay, set out for the upper reaches of the territory in order " to establish a system of trade with the Indians." [16] Within a short time, from its headquarters on Mackinac Island, the American Fur Company controlled the trade in the rich fur districts of the Northwest.[17]

Although the American Fur Company maintained an agency in the city, Detroit remained the emporium of the independent trader.

Local merchants conducted operations in conjunction with their business of supplying the countryside with groceries, drygoods, and manufactured articles. Sometimes they outfitted several parties with trade goods and sent them into the Indian country to bid for furs, but they gradually reduced such operations as the competition offered by the American Fur Company increased. The bulk of the furs shipped from the West in the years that followed came from the depots of this great organization.[18]

Prior to the settlement and development of the hinterland, however, the fur trade was of immense importance to Detroit. For a number of years furs and peltries were about the only products of the territory exported to the East. It has been pointed out that the returns from their sale enabled Detroit merchants to pay for much of the essential goods brought to the city. By 1820 it was estimated that as many as a thousand persons were employed in the trade in Michigan.[19] Nevertheless, it was apparent to many that the trade contributed little to the permanent prosperity of Detroit and the Michigan Territory. Great numbers of the French populace permitted their lands to lie fallow year after year while they pursued the more alluring employment found in the fur trade. Thus, while this trade apparently brought great wealth to the city, the neglect of agriculture necessitated a continued dependence upon the farmers of Ohio and Pennsylvania. In deprecating this situation a contributor to the *Gazette* wrote in 1817: "It is evident that if it were not for the article of fur, the landed property, and its remnant of wealth, must very soon be transferred to the citizens of Ohio." [20] Four years later when a rise in the price of furs produced increased activity among the fur buyers in Detroit, the editor of the *Gazette* declared:

> This, in these hard times, is something to console the good people of this territory—for it must be allowed that the amount of furs, annually collected and sold by the traders and inhabitants, is very considerable in our list of articles for transportation—indeed, fur is almost the only article

worthy of note. Yet, how much more consoling it would be, could we assure ourselves that even a small portion of the amount of our fur could return to the territory in *cash*, to be expended in the erection of mills and useful machinery and the making of roads and bridges. Instead of this all the fur that is collected by our merchants go as [*sic*] towards the payment of debts contracted for *foreign fabrics*, or in exchange for them; and not only the fur, but almost all the money that they receive from the improvident consumers of these fabrics. We may with propriety (in relation to the effect on the immediate interests of the people of the territory) call everything foreign that is not made in the territory. The time is not far distant, however, when we will know and pursue our true interests. . . .[21]

Despite the energy and industry displayed by the local merchants in the pursuit of the trade, the results were not always pleasant. Prices in the fur market fluctuated so rapidly that it was almost impossible for the local buyer to purchase with confidence unless he had the latest information from New York.[22] Trade goods purchased at high market prices in 1815 and 1816 quickly depreciated in value when cheaper European merchandise once again reached the interior.[23] As competition increased, prices were reduced and profits diminished.[24] Williams wrote to his agent in New York in the spring of 1817: " The last sales of furs fell very far short of my expectations. I lost several hundred dollars on that parcel." [25] Some of the merchants lacked the means to continue in business after suffering severe losses.[26] The *Gazette*, in a long review of the fur trade, asked rhetorically:

But where is the man who has grown rich by the fur trade? Scarcely an individual can be found, in the long period which has elapsed since the British acquired possession of this country, who has not ultimately been injured by it; and not one remains in or about this place, whose prosperity can be fairly attributed to these enterprises.[27]

From April 1, 1817 to March 31, 1818, 1,378 packs of furs, valued at $110,240 were exported from Detroit.[28] It was estimated that $300,000 in furs arrived and departed from the city during the summer of 1821.[29] Gradually, however, the collections diminished. As the Indians departed from the lands they had sold to the United States, and as the eastern farmers entered them and cleared them the fur-bearers disappeared. The furs arriving in Detroit in 1821 were largely from the northern parts of the territory. Williams wrote to his agent regarding the sale of his furs: "These furs are almost all from Saguina [sic] and its vicinity. You must know that muskrats are exceedingly scarce this year. In places where thousands were killed 2 or 3 years ago not one is to be found now."[30] By 1825 the fur trade was but of minor importance to most of the merchants of Detroit. The settlement and development of the hinterland had produced a more diversified trade. The decline in the fur trade was demonstrated by Williams' shipments: in 1817 he collected fifty-five packs and forwarded them to the East; in 1825 he sent only four.[31]

Except for the fur trade the only other commercial opportunity in Detroit until the outbreak of the War of 1812 was that of provisioning the small garrison stationed there and of providing for the personal wants of the soldiers.[32] It was the government disbursements for the support of the armed forces and the Indian Department which enabled Detroit to offset its unfavorable trade balance.[33] During the years immediately following the war the city was more than ever dependent upon these expenditures. While the garrison was gradually reduced new posts were established at Chicago, Green Bay, and Mackinac.[34] Most of the provisions for these troops were sent from Detroit,[35] but only a small portion of them were produced in the neighborhood of the city. This situation led to the development of a three-cornered trade, which was of vital importance to the commercial interests in Detroit. Merchants bartered their goods for the barrelled fish, apples, and cider which some of the more industrious French

residents brought to market. These productions found a ready
market in Ohio and were taken in payment for much of the flour,
meat, whiskey, and dairy produce imported from that state. The
merchants subsequently sold the greater part of these imports to
the army contractor for the subsistence of the troops at the various
garrisons and were paid in cash or in credit instruments which
they could use to pay for the goods imported from the East.[36]

The requirements of the Detroit garrison alone were considerable. In 1818 the War Department asked for proposals to furnish
it with 1,378 barrels of pork, 2,871 bushels of peas or beans,
3,691 barrels of flour, 643 barrels of whiskey, 230 hundredweight
of soap, 9,645 pounds of candles, 402 bushels of salt, and 6,430
gallons of vinegar.[37] In addition to expenditures for food the
War Department also made disbursements for transporting troops
and supplies and for furnishing the garrison with "fuel, forage
and straw." [38]

The money paid out to the troops in Detroit amounted to a
substantial sum each year. For a long time the retail merchants
had depended upon this for a large part of their business and
welcomed the opportunity of exchanging their merchandise for
the ready cash of the soldiers. After the war they anticipated a
continuance of this business, but much to their dismay, in 1816
the Secretary of War appointed a sutler for the post. Under the
terms of his agreement with the War Department the sutler was
granted a virtual monopoly of the soldiers' trade and their contingent expenditures. The merchants protested this action, claiming that their sufferings and losses during the war entitled them
to a portion of the trade, but their remonstrances were of no avail.
In summing up the situation the *Gazette* remarked:

> There was a time when public disbursements were essenti-
> ally beneficial to the inhabitants at large of this territory; but
> that has passed away. The system that now prevails, and has
> prevailed for a year past, is only beneficial to a few, as the

chief amount of the money destined for the pay of the soldiers is transferred from the paymaster's hands to those of the sutlers, and from thence is remitted direct to some of our commercial cities for supplies of such articles of merchandise as are in demand for the army.[39]

Any reduction in the numbers of the troops at Detroit served to decrease federal expenditures in the city. In 1817 the garrison numbered " about 400," which was a far cry from the 1,500 troops stationed at Detroit, or in the neighborhood of the city, in 1815.[40] When it was rumored in 1819 that the troops were to be removed from the post, the *Gazette* protested vehemently. While it did not fear for the security of the territory, it felt that its apparent defenseless state would deter settlers from coming, and that " some, whose fears from Indians have no influence over them," would " refuse to become settlers in consequence of seeing those resources removed, which offered themselves through the disbursement of public monies—resources all important to the emigrant at his out-set in a new country." [41] Finally, in 1823 most of the troops in Detroit were sent to the Atlantic coast, and a skeleton force remained in the cantonment to watch over the arsenal and to guard United States property.[42] When, after a few years, the military reserve was completely abandoned and turned over to the city, it marked the end of a field of endeavor that had constituted a substantial pillar in the early economy of Detroit.

The sale of public lands in Michigan in the summer of 1818 was a turning point in the economic development of the territory. It presaged the fulfillment of the hopes of those who looked to the American settlement of the area as the basis for its future prosperity. A more energetic agricultural class would tend to relieve Detroit from dependence upon Ohio for foodstuffs, and would provide a better market for the absorption of local manufactures and imported merchandise. Elkanah Watson, visiting in the city at the time, wrote:

It is impossible for an old traveler to look upon the existing
condition of Michigan and not be impressed with a conviction
of the great and rapid changes which await the territory.
It is destined to soon emerge from its present social and
agricultural depression into a great state, rich, populous, and
progressive, and enjoying all the refinements and elegancies
of civilized society. Detroit will rank among the great cities
of America. Agriculture, the basis of all public prosperity,
is now lamentably debased in general, scarcely advanced
from the point it occupied centuries ago. The depression of
agriculture necessarily bears down the interests of commerce,
for in a country like this, where is commerce without agriculture? [43]

Even with an excellent home market, there had been but small
improvement in agriculture since the close of the war. The *habitants* lacked the ability and the initiative to take advantage of
the great demand for foodstuffs. A contributor to the *Gazette*
suggested that they study the more practical methods of agriculture
being introduced into the territory by the Americans. He further
suggested that the local farmers " form themselves into a Society
for the Improvement and Encouragement of Agriculture." [44] The
suggestion seemed to find favor with the more progressive element
in the city, for in November, 1817 the Michigan Agricultural
Society was organized.[45] In an attempt to stimulate the flagging
endeavors of the French farmers, the society offered prizes for
the best efforts in agriculture and in stock raising for the year
1818; in some of the categories the competition extended until
1821.[46] The editor of the *Gazette*, thereafter, used every possible
means at his command to enlighten the French and to better their
methods of husbandry. Week after week there appeared in the
columns of the paper treatises and communications in regard to
agricultural improvement.[47] Despite these efforts most of the
French farmers were content to continue their improvident existence—and, consequently, food costs in Detroit remained at a high

level. In the summer of 1817 wheat and corn sold at $2.00 per bushel, oats $1.00, and potatoes $1.25. Flour was marketed at from $12.00 to $13.00 a barrel. Pork cost from $26.00 to $30.00 a barrel; beef $6.00 per hundredweight.[48]

Those citizens of the territory interested in promoting its well-being had endeavored to refute the Tiffin report, and their activities in this regard were largely responsible for the opening of the land sales. When this was accomplished they redoubled their efforts to induce better-equipped farmers to migrate to Michigan. The editorial column of the *Gazette* became a virtual prospectus of the opportunities to be found in the territory. It asserted that produce could be raised in Michigan as well as in any other part of the Union, and that there was no part of the western country where it would command such good returns. It pointed out that if essential foods could be raised in Ohio and transported to Detroit at a profit to the farmer, they could certainly be produced to greater advantage on the fertile lands in the neighborhood of the city. The editor claimed that if the money paid out yearly to Ohio farmers for furnishing the city with " the actual necessities of life" were to be divided among two hundred farmers in Michigan, " it would not only enrich them, but materially assist every part of [the] community." To lend credence to his declaration, he added: " At present we can without fear of contradiction assert that there are not TWELVE good practical farmers in the territory."[49]

The nation-wide economic depression of 1819 tended to limit the migration of American farmers to Michigan.[50] While food costs diminished greatly in the more populous areas of the country, they continued excessively high in Detroit. The *Gazette* complained of the necessity of paying " *in these hard times* . . . the same price for eatables, that we gave two years ago, when we saw five dollars put into our pockets oftener than we now see one dollar placed there."[51] The few American farmers who had arrived in the territory had not sufficiently developed their holdings to make their presence felt. They continued to arrive in small numbers, but as the price of farm produce remained at a low level in the East, many found it impossible to raise the funds necessary for removing to Michigan, and purchasing farms there. In the fall of 1819 the *Chautaqua* [New York] *Gazette* reported that " first quality wheat," which had ranged in price from $1.00 to $2.50 per bushel during the previous three years, did not find a ready sale even when it was offered at 37½ cents per bushel.[52] While prices rose gradually in the ensuing months, it was not until the fall of 1821 that they approached their pre-depression level. Under the heading, " Good News," and in bold type, the *Gazette* published an article from an Albany paper which stated that, in consequence of reports that southern wheat crops would be small and that those in Europe had failed, the price of wheat had mounted to more than $2.00 per bushel. While subsequent reports minimized the extent of the crop damage and prices diminished somewhat, it betokened well for Detroit and Michigan Territory. With their augmented incomes it was believed that a substantial number of eastern farmers would dispose of their property and set out for the West.[53]

On the whole, however, the prices of farm productions remained far below those of former years. The appreciation of the currency during the depression was largely responsible for the reduction, and time alone could heal the wounds caused by inflationary practices. By 1822 the farmer was fairly well reconciled to the new standard of values, for while his income was lower than before, the purchasing power of the dollar was greater. Williams visited central New York in the summer of 1822, and after noting conditions there, wrote to an associate in Detroit:

> Wheat was worth as high as 6/ [75 cents per bushel] here this spring but will not bring more than 4/ [50 cents] at present owing to the reduction in the price of flour in New York. Notwithstanding the reduced price of produce the country seems to be in a very flourishing condition and

improvements of every sort progressing on—yet real estate and lands have greatly depreciated in value. There is a number of able and respectable farmers in this neighborhood that are desirous of selling their property with the avowed object of moving to Michigan.[54]

The action of Congress in reducing the price of land in the public domain and providing for the relief of those who had made purchases at the higher rate was in line with its policy of curbing inflation and stabilizing the currency. The reduction of the minimum purchase from 160 acres to 80 was welcomed by the conservative farmer of small means.

In consequence of the shortage of money and the depressed state of affairs in the West, prices dropped considerably in Detroit between the spring of 1819 and the summer of 1821. The *Gazette* was quick to point out that the depreciation could not be attributed to the "increased industry of the *Michigan* farmers," and the abundance with which they had filled the local market. Most of them continued their haphazard methods of agriculture, and such was their indolence that while it was estimated that there was sufficient land cleared in the territory to sustain a population six times its number, they permitted Ohio farmers to sell thousands of barrels of animal and vegetable foods in the city yearly. "Since navigation opened this spring," said the *Gazette*, "there have been upwards of fifteen arrivals of vessels, in the port of Detroit, laden with produce to feed the farmers and other inhabitants of this territory." [55]

The lack of agricultural staples for exportation was detrimental to the prosperous development of the region. To offset its unfavorable trade balance it was deemed necessary to promote the production of those commodities which could bear the expense of transportation to eastern markets. In the spring of 1822 the *Gazette* declared: "Our country is too far inland to admit of our growing grain with a view to exportation; but there are other crops, far more valuable, and of a less bulky nature, to which our climate, soil and situation are eminently adapted." [56] For some time it had advocated the cultivation of flax, hemp, tobacco, and currant wine, and had recommended the raising of sheep for their wool as a profitable enterprise. It pointed out that the markets for these articles were more stable than the grains and that their bulk was so small in comparison with their value that they could " always bear transportation to a distance." [57] When American farmers began arriving in larger numbers in the spring of 1822, the paper attempted to interest them in the cultivation of export crops. It urged them to vary their productions, for while they undoubtedly would find the raising of grains and meat stock profitable, they would " be compelled to indulge in fewer luxuries, and the products of their labor [would] not afford a foundation for that active commerce, and profitable intercourse with the other states, and with foreign nations, which a good system of agriculture would inevitably create." The editor was particularly interested in the raising of hemp as an export staple. " Ten thousand acres only, of Michigan land, devoted to the growing of hemp," he predicted, " would bring into the territory a million of dollars annually." [58] Some hemp and a little tobacco were raised in Michigan during 1822, but the new farmers evidently devoted most of their energies to clearing their lands and raising grains and vegetables. [59]

Food prices rose sharply in Detroit during the spring of 1823. Between February and June the price of flour increased from $4.50 per barrel to as high as $7.00, and other essentials rose in like proportion. The *Gazette* claimed that it knew of no other place that had experienced such a great rise in food costs. Notwithstanding the fact that there was an increase in the production of foodstuffs in Michigan during the year, and that large importations continued to arrive from Ohio, prices remained high in consequence of the small amount of produce for sale and the general belief that there was not a sufficient supply to last the winter. The *Gazette* attributed the shortage to the extraordinary

demand created by the "great additions" to the population of
the territory during the year.[60] By 1824 the American farmers
in the hinterland were producing substantial amounts of wheat
and other grains, but, despite their efforts, there was no surplus
to ship to the Detroit market. The *Gazette* explained the situation:

> Three years ago we were of the opinion that in 1824, the
> inhabitants of Michigan, as well as the troops stationed on
> the upper Lakes, would be supplied with provisions of all
> kinds by the industry and enterprise of our farmers, without
> the assistance of those of Ohio and the western parts of
> Pennsylvania. But we were mistaken, and it is now pretty
> well ascertained that the influx of emigrants to this territory
> will continue to render our trade with Ohio, in a measure
> necessary to ourselves and profitable to her farmers, for some
> time to come. It must be obvious, from the experience which
> we have had that now is the time for our farmers to exert
> themselves.[61]

The prospect of an early completion of the Erie Canal was
influential in changing the attitude of Michigan farmers regarding
the production of grains. Experienced producers estimated that
wheat could be raised profitably in Michigan for fifty cents per
bushel, and they began to cultivate it extensively. The high price
of wheat and flour in the home market promised to continue for
some time, but even after it was satisfied, the surplus could be
transported advantageously to the East via Lake Erie and the Erie
Canal. Aided by favorable weather, bumper crops of wheat and
other grains were raised in Michigan in 1825. The *Gazette*
asserted, however, that the new county of Washtenaw would have
no surplus of wheat even though it would produce a large crop.
"So great is the emigration to that county," it explained, "that
it is supposed the whole will be wanted for seed, and that every
bushel will be worth a dollar or more, at the barns." [62] In December, 1825, however, the paper took notice of an event which was

of momentous import to the future of Detroit and the Michigan Territory. Under the heading "Better Prospects," it said:

> We mention, as a singular fact, and entirely new in this territory, that a wagon-load of FLOUR arrived in town last week from the interior. It was made at Col. Mack's mills, in Pontiac, and we understand that there are several hundred barrels there which will be brought in soon. This is the first season in which the farmers of Oakland have been able to raise grain enough to supply themselves and the emigrants.
>
> It will not be long before Washtenaw, Lenawee, and Macomb will also be able to raise enough to supply themselves—and they can easily send their surplus, through the canal to our neighbors in New York—or to our neighbors in the West Indies, when the improvements of the St. Lawrence are completed.[63]

While the orchards in the neighborhood of Detroit had long been noted for their productivity and the flavor of their fruits, they had been sorely neglected by their French owners. Apples, pears, and peaches grew abundantly. An observer claimed that practically every farm contained an orchard of mature trees capable of producing from one hundred to one thousand bushels of fruit annually. Cider, in particular, found a ready market in the newly-settled regions of Ohio and Indiana, for the orchards there had not yet reached the productive stage. Notwithstanding this demand, and the great need for export commodities, some of the *habitants* permitted the fruit to rot on the ground or to be eaten by the hogs. They were urged to take better care of their trees and to perpetuate them by planting and caring for the shoots.[64] While the exportation of cider and apples increased considerably during 1818,[65] an observer in 1819 took note of the dead and decaying fruit trees "at almost every farmhouse," and warned that if the orchards were not given better care, the farmers would "lose one of the very few articles they have to barter." [66] The Michigan Agricultural Society attempted to encourage the production of fruits in the region by offering as a premium " a piece of PLATE, worth twenty-five dollars" to the individual "having the largest and best nursery, containing the greatest variety of choicest fruit trees, in the year 1821." [67] The French, evidently, took as little interest in nurseries as they did in their orchards, but the incoming Americans secured seeds and shoots from the trees and planted them on their farms in the hinterland, thus assuring the perpetuity of valuable strains and laying the foundation for a profitable industry.[68]

Stock raising in the neighborhood of Detroit was slow to recover from the crippling effects of the war. For years thereafter, the scarcity of meat and dairy products constituted a major problem in the city. Although large numbers of cattle, swine, and sheep had been brought to Detroit in 1815, the demand for meat on both sides of the river was so great that few animals were kept for breeding purposes. Cattle were reported to be " very dear" in the spring of 1816; beef sold for twelve cents a pound and pork for thirty dollars per barrel. Butter and cheese were extremely scarce.[69] Barrelled beef and pork continued to arrive in the city by open boat and sailing vessel from ports in Ohio, while meat stock came by the tortuous land route. Despite these importations General Macomb informed the Secretary of War in the summer of 1816 that the army contractor would have difficulty in supplying the troops with fresh meat.[70] The *Gazette* declared in its first issue, July 25, 1817, that seventeen hundred head of cattle had arrived from Ohio since the month of May; it predicted, however, that it would not be long before there would be a surplus of cattle in the region, for local production was rapidly increasing.[71] But production could not keep pace with the demands created by the mounting population of the city and the desire of American farmers to supply their farms with live-stock. As late as 1825 the *Gazette* noted: " Droves of cattle are almost daily arriving in this place, from Ohio and Kentucky, to supply our new farmers. They sell at a high price." [72]

The scarcity of meat in Detroit during these years would have been more serious had it not been for the large quantities of excellent fish taken from waters in the vicinity of the city each year. Although the Detroit River yielded fish of many varieties, the whitefish and the lake trout were the most abundant and the most desirable. Beginning about the middle of October each year and continuing until the first of December, whitefish appeared by the thousands in the river, and the French and Indians caught as many as they wished with spear or net. The *habitants* cured the fish for their own use and also sold them to the townspeople. They were taken in such large numbers, and the local market was so limited, that in 1818 fresh fish could be purchased at the wharf for fifty cents per hundred pounds; cleaned and salted they sold for three dollars per barrel.[73] The difficulty of forwarding fish from the seaboard to the West led to the sampling of the fresh-water varieties and the development of the Detroit fisheries. Evidently the residents of Ohio were among the first to realize the potentialities of the fishing industry, for by 1817 they were casting their nets in the waters of the river and sending hundreds of barrels of salted fish to their home markets.[74] The *Gazette* expressed its regret that Detroiters—despite the city's great need for export products—displayed such little interest in the industry and permitted strangers to carry away " that which ought every year . . . [to] throw considerable sums of money into the pockets of the citizens." [75] The high price of salt and the expense of transportation contributed to the slow development of the industry.[76]

By 1820, however, the people of the West were developing a taste for lake fish, and the demand for them increased steadily. During that year, on eleven fishing grounds within eighteen miles of Detroit, 1,385 barrels of fish were prepared for export, and about 500 barrels for home consumption. Although Detroit was taking more interest in the industry, two-thirds of the fish shipped to other markets were exported by Ohio fishermen. With these facts at hand the *Gazette* once again attempted to spur Detroit citizens to greater efforts. " Surely," it remarked,

> if persons can come from the state of Ohio, a distance of two or three hundred miles, leaving their usual business, and realize sufficient profit from fishing, notwithstanding the disadvantages under which they must labor at a distance from home, to induce their returning almost every season, our own citizens should reflect that they too might make it a business individually profitable, and give labor to many persons who, during the fishing season, are destitute of employment.[77]

The paper urged the fishermen to use more care in preparing the fish for market, pointing out that the future of the industry depended upon the good quality of the product and that if the fish were not properly handled and barrelled, great loss might result.[78] In 1822 a greater number of persons were engaged in the industry than in any former year, and it was reported that a greater quantity of fish was taken. It was claimed that one Detroiter caught 1,200 barrels off Hog Island (Belle Isle), and that they were valued at from four to five dollars per barrel in the local market.[79]

A group of Detroit residents organized a company in 1823 which proposed to develop the industry by expanding operations and improving the methods of preparing the fish for market.[80] Much to the dismay of the local interests the fish failed to run in large numbers, and not more than a thousand barrels were taken in the river during the whole season. The *Gazette* noted: " The country is not half supplied, and large sums of money, brought here to be paid for fish, have been taken from the territory." [81] In the fall of 1824, however, the fish appeared in their usual numbers, and great activity was displayed in catching them and preparing them for market. It was estimated that between four and five thousand barrels were put up during the season, and that they would be worth between twenty-five and thirty thousand dollars. While this "handsome income" contributed greatly to the economic advancement of the territory, it continued to be shared "in a considerable degree" with fisherman from Ohio. "But they are welcome to come," said the *Gazette*, "until we are sufficiently numerous to man every ground from Grosse Isle to Lake Huron." [82]

In the spring of 1825 the Legislative Council of the territory took steps to regulate fishing in the waters under its jurisdiction. By the terms of the act it passed, it was illegal to use nets longer than forty-five fathoms; fishing with nets on Sunday was prohibited; no attempt could be made to direct the natural progress of the fish by artificial means; and fishermen were forbidden to operate in waters fronting the land of any person without his permission—except in the channel of the rivers. The act provided penalties for any infringement of the regulations. [83]

Meanwhile, the market for whitefish had widened. Detroiters had aided in the extension by forwarding barrels of fish to the East as gifts for their friends. [84] The opening of the Erie Canal further reduced the cost of transportation, and the great migration to the West that preceded and followed its completion produced an increasing demand for fish. The *Gazette* claimed in the fall of 1825 that "from Ohio and the western towns of New-York" there had come orders for thousands of barrels. [85] Between forty and fifty seines were actively engaged in the Detroit River, and it was estimated that the catch from these waters alone would exceed three thousand barrels. [86] During the years that followed, operations continued to expand, and barrelled fish became one of the foremost export staples of the territory. [87]

The most significant development in the economic advancement of Detroit in the decade following the war was the growth of a substantial inland trade. As early as 1820 visitors to the city predicted that like Pittsburgh, Cincinnati, and St. Louis it would become the outfitting post for a wide area. [88] With the decline of the fur trade and the reduction of the market afforded by the garrison in the city, Detroit merchants found deliverance in a growing local trade and in fulfilling the needs of the multitude of new settlers swarming into the hinterland. They imported most of their merchandise from New York City, ordering in sufficient quantities to last the succeeding winter, for due to the freezing of the Lakes and the difficulties of land transportation the city was virtually isolated during the winter months.[89] Each store stocked a great variety of goods, there being but small trend at this time toward specialization. At one of these establishments, a customer could usually satisfy his needs, whether in drygoods, crockery, imported foodstuffs, liquors, or country produce.[90]

Detroit, as capital of the territory, was the seat of administration for the Indian Department in Michigan, and for the vast unorganized regions bordering it on the northwest. Cass acted as Superintendent of Indian Affairs for the department in addition to his duties as Governor.[91] Large numbers of Indians annually visited the city.[92] Out of its contingent fund the department spent considerable amounts of money to supply the visitors with presents and to maintain its office, and a large part of the merchandise was purchased of local merchants.[93] Most of the supplies and trade goods for the exploring expedition into the Northwest in 1820 was furnished by Detroit merchants.[94] They also supplied much of the merchandise used in negotiating treaties with the Indians.[95] These expenditures by the federal government were of great importance to the commercial interests in the city during the early twenties, for, generally speaking, it was a period of economic stagnation.

Mercantile establishments in the city multiplied as the population of the territory increased. By 1824 there were five wharves and storehouses, thirty stores, and thirteen groceries catering to the inhabitants of the hinterland and of the shorelands on both sides of the river, in addition to supplying the local market.[96] Advertisements in the *Gazette* announced the opening of several new stores in 1824 and 1825.[97]

Some Detroit citizens engaged in the forwarding and commission trade either in conjunction with their regular business
or as a separate pursuit. They received consignments of merchandise from abroad and disposed of them in the local market
or in the hinterland on a commission basis. With the growth of
the Detroit market this trade became more brisk. James Abbott,
the local postmaster, carried on an extensive business as proprietor
of the "Commission House" and sold a wide variety of merchandise.[98] In January, 1825, Williams noted that business was
not very satisfactory "in consequence of the number of stores
and large amount of goods" brought to the city.[99] Nevertheless,
when the steamship *Superior* arrived in Detroit the following
spring, it was "deeply laden with goods for the merchants."[100]
The estimated 50 per cent increase in the population of the territory during 1825 offered new opportunities for the commission
trade.[101]

The scarcity of money during these years was instrumental in
forcing a continued dependence upon the barter system to facilitate local transactions. Furs were received on a par with cash,[102]
but their gradual disappearance from the Detroit region, together
with the increase in population and the great demand for foodstuffs, brought other items to the fore. In 1817 a local tailor
offered to sell a span of horses, a wagon, two carts, harnesses,
and a sleigh "cheap for cash or country produce."[103] Another
citizen advertised that he would accept corn, flour, and oats in
exchange for 2,000 pounds of maple sugar.[104] At the beginning
of the fishing season in 1819 Williams had 400 fish barrels and
89 barrels of salt which he wished to trade "for salted whitefish,
at the market price."[105] In an attempt to increase its circulation,
the editor of the *Gazette* wrote in 1821: "Farmers who wish to
become subscribers and who are prevented on account of the
scarcity of money, are again informed that all kinds of grain,
butter and cheese will be received in payment."[106] In 1822 a local
merchant advertised "all or any" of his merchandise for sale

" at reduced prices for wheat, rye, corn, flour, beans, oats, barley, or hides." [107] The proprietor of an establishment opening for business in January, 1824 announced that he would " receive in exchange for goods purchased of him the following commodities, to wit, cash, grain of all kinds, furs, ginseng, beeswax, and hides." [108]

While the residents of the interior had few surplus cereal foods for barter prior to 1826, there were certain products of the field and forest which they could trade for necessary supplies. It was reported that most of the farmers in the newly settled parts of the territory had " domesticated from five to fifty, and, in some instances, a hundred hives of bees." [109] The high prices paid for imported sugars in Detroit created a good market for the maple sugar that the farmer might produce in excess of his own needs.[110] The ashes of the trees burned to make new clearings, as well as those of the hearth, were much in demand by soap manufacturers, and Detroit merchants were eager to obtain them.[111]

There was but small advancement in the manufacture of goods for the home market during the decade 1815-1825. " The manner of living necessarily adopted by the first French settlers of this territory, and the characteristics of the subsequent generations," said the *Gazette*, " have rendered their wants as to manufactures very limited." They depended almost wholly upon the merchants to supply their needs.[112] On other frontiers in the United States the family ordinarily produced much of its own clothing, but home manufactures were practically non-existent among the *habitants*. In a commentary on the situation in 1816 Cass declared: " The spinning wheel and the loom are unknown in the country." He claimed that in the past the French had thrown away the wool of the sheep, and he presumed: ". . . even now . . . a pound of wool is not manufactured in the territory by any person of Canadian descent." [113] As late as 1821 the *Gazette* asserted:

There are not three families that manufacture their wearing

apparel—and it is believed that there are not five looms in the territory.

There is not a carding machine or fulling mill within, perhaps, a hundred miles of Detroit.[114]

With the arrival in the territory of the more talented and energetic Americans, home manufactures increased. The firm of Jackson & Town established a fulling mill " at the River Raisin " in 1823 where home-manufactured cloth would be " fulled, dyed, sheared, pressed and finished in the best manner." [115] In 1824 Eldred & French began the operation of a carding machine in Detroit.[116]

The lack of water power in the vicinity of Detroit proved a decided handicap to its industrial development, for it prohibited the utilization of power machinery.[117] Steam power could not be introduced, for, if wood was used as fuel, it was too expensive, and coal was unavailable.[118] While the French had long depended upon windmills for grinding their grains, and a great number of them lined " both banks of the river Detroit," the flour produced in this manner was never " considered very good." [119] Prior to 1818, for want of sawmills, lumber had to be cut by hand or imported.[120] In the spring of 1818 Henry Conner announced the completion of a gristmill and a sawmill on a stream five miles above the city, and by the end of the next year two gristmills and two sawmills were in operation in Pontiac.[121] The demand for a more efficient way of making flour in Detroit led to the erection in 1821 of " an excellent team gristmill, with two run of stones " by Abraham Edwards. The mill was powered by four oxen, and the flour it produced was described as " the best that has ever been offered in this market." [122] In the summer of 1825 another gristmill went into operation on the River Rouge, the miller advertising that he would return " a barrel of flour for five bushels of good wheat, weighing sixty pounds per bushel—the owner of the wheat furnishing the barrel." [123] About the same time a

factory for the manufacture of woolen cloth was established at
Pontiac, the proprietors advertising that they would

> receive wool in the fleece, and manufacture it into cloth, for
> one half of the same; or into cloth three-fourths of a yard
> wide, for sixty-two and a half cents per yard; if wider, in
> proportion.
>
> Wool delivered David Cooper, merchant in Detroit [would]
> be received and manufactured on the same conditions, with
> the addition of transportation of the wool to Pontiac.[124]

As early as 1821 the editor of the *Gazette* stated prophetically:
" The market for the staple productions of the western country
must be found, not in Europe, nor in our own large cities, but
in towns nearer home, in supplying manufacturers, who must very
soon fabricate seven-tenths of the articles we now import, or we
must give up the use of them." [125] Among the articles it felt
might be manufactured profitably in the city and territory were
potash, iron, glass, woolen goods, linen goods, rope, sail-cloth,
tar, salt, oil, and distilled spirits.[126] A few small handicraft shops
were in existence prior to 1821, but the quantity and value of
their products were small.[127] There was a shortage of practical
craftsmen and mechanics in the territory, as well as of practical
farmers. Evans, visiting Detroit in 1818, observed: " Here . . .
all mechanical trades would be promptly patronized. Various
articles of American manufacture are sent to this place from the
city of New York, and meet here a market affording great profits.
Joiners, brickmakers, shoemakers, and almost all other mechanics
would obtain here ready employment and good wages." [128] A
census of the city in 1819 revealed that there were 174 mechanics
residing within its confines, listed as follows:

> Blacksmiths, 18; Watchmakers, Silversmiths and Jewelers,
> 7; Gunsmith, 1; Carpenters and Joiners, 60; Coopers, 6;
> Cabinetmakers, 3: Coach and Chaise maker, 1; Wheelwrights,
> 5; Tanners and Curriers, 3: Saddlers and Harness makers, 5;

Shoemakers, 12; Masons and Bricklayers, 23; Tailors, 18; Hatters, 6; Tinner, 1; Painters, 3; Printers, 3.[129]

Evidently, not all of these craftsmen found profitable employment in the city, especially those engaged in the manufacture of goods for the local market. In the spring of 1819 a contributor to the *Gazette* over the signature, " Mechanic of Detroit," wrote:

> The practice of the mercantile part of the community, of purchasing in the states, and bringing to this territory large quantities of articles, which can be made within it, has been greatly injurious to the *general* prosperity, and if not discontinued, will ultimately be of essential injury to their own. . . . It is proven true by a glance at our city which, considering its population and its wants, presents fewer, and a far more destitute body of mechanics, than, perhaps, can be found in any place in the United States containing an equal number of inhabitants.

He claimed that hatters, shoemakers, saddle and harness makers, and various other mechanics found it difficult to become established in the city, even though their products were as low-priced and as fashionable as those imported by the merchants from New York. Some who had recently arrived found their prospects so poor that they refused to remain in the city, and those who remained were producing but a small proportion of the goods they were capable of turning out. He concluded:

> Every candid and liberal merchant, having at heart the general prosperity, will, I am convinced, upon reflection, decide that the interests of the mechanic should be supported —and the best way to do this is to assist him by creating a demand for his work.[130]

Those engaged in the building trades were more fortunate in finding employment; fifty-one buildings were erected in the city during 1818, including a stone jail and a large stone church.[131]

There was evidently a wide demand for their services in 1819, despite the nation-wide economic depresssion, for the *Gazette* noted that higher wages were paid in Detroit than in other parts of the country: "We pay a common laborer *one dollar* a day; a mason or a carpenter gets from *twelve shillings* to *two dollars twenty five cents* a day, and some get $2.50." [132] Some of the mechanics, particularly blacksmiths, wheelwrights, carpenters, coopers, and gunsmiths, received considerable business from the Indian Department in the manufacture and repair of equipment presented to the various tribes.[133]

The prospect of cheap lands in the hinterland together with the good market for agricultural products undoubtedly drew many of the mechanics to farms in the interior. Others sought a better field for their talents in the new towns that developed after 1818.[134] The construction of new buildings declined somewhat after 1818, averaging only nineteen per year during the next five years.[135] A census taken at the close of 1823 revealed that many of those formerly engaged in the building trades must have turned to the farm or found employment elsewhere. There was but little change in the numbers employed in other trades. The census indicated that there were in the city at the time:

> . . . 1 engraver and miniature painter, 3 watchmakers and jewelers, 4 cabinetmakers, 5 bakers, 5 stonemasons, 5 tailors, 3 painters and glaziers, 2 chair makers, 10 house joiners and carpenters, 2 hatters, 5 blacksmiths, 3 gunsmiths, 1 wheel maker, 6 butchers, 1 saddle and harness maker, 2 tanners and curriers, 5 shoemakers, 2 dyers and scourers, 1 wagon and sleigh maker, 2 coopers, and 3 barbers.[136]

While the shortage of skilled construction labor during this period was at times a matter of concern, it did not become a real problem until 1825.[137] The flood of newcomers to the territory in that year, and the resultant expansion of commercial interests, created a vast demand for new buildings. Although fifty-eight buildings

were erected during the year there was need for more.[138] The
editor of the *Herald* asserted that rents were high in consequence
of the demand for building space, and he expressed the belief
that money could not be invested more profitably in any other
part of the United States than it could be in buildings in Detroit.
He further asserted:

> The demand for mechanic labor, and labor of every descrip-
> tion connected with building, is greater than can be supplied,
> which has the effect of enhancing wages and retarding the
> improvement of the city. Carpenters, masons, brick-makers,
> and common laborers from abroad will undoubtedly, for years
> to come, find employment and good wages, not only in
> Detroit but in the interior of the territory. Every industrious
> mechanic, who comes here from abroad, is a valuable acquisi-
> tion and is of more immediate utility than a ship load of
> lawyers and doctors.[139]

While a few manufacturing enterprises began operations in
Detroit after 1820, by 1825 they had scarcely risen above the level
of handicraft shops. James Abbott announced the completion of
the " Detroit Brewery " in 1823, and said that he would " constantly keep on hand a supply of beer and porter " which he would
" sell on as reasonable terms as possible, considering the high
price and scarcity of materials." [140] In the same year Peter Parent
opened a " Cabinet Making Business," advertising that the style
and quality of his furniture, together with its low price, would
render it unnecessary for the people of the territory " to send to
distant towns for their furniture." [141] A tinware " factory " was
established the next year, its proprietors claiming that they would
sell their products 30 to 50 per cent cheaper than they had been
selling theretofore, in addition to saving the risk and expense of
transportation.[142]

Despite the importance of Detroit as a lake port, it had taken
little interest in shipbuilding during the period of American occupation. In fact, as late as 1825, Michigan Territory could not

boast the construction of a single " decent vessel," most of the
ships owned in Detroit having been built in Ohio or Pennsylvania.
The winter of 1825-26 witnessed the commencement of the
industry in Michigan, when a Detroit merchant contracted for the
construction of a " schooner of the first class " near Mt. Clemens.[143]
Thus was born an industry which was to reach large proportions
in succeeding years.

CHAPTER V—NOTES

[1] Cass to Crawford, May 31, 1816, Clarence Edwin Carter, ed. and comp., *The
Territorial Papers of the United States* (10 vols.; Washington, 1934-1942), X, 642.

[2] Macomb to Major-General Brown, June 21, 1816, " Alexander Macomb Letterbook, 1807-1819 " (Typescript, Burton Historical Collection, Detroit Public Library;
hereafter cited as B. H. C.).

[3] Boyd & Suydam to Williams, July 26, October 7, 1815, and January 6, 1818,
" John R. Williams Papers " (MS, B. H. C.).

[4] Oliver Granger to Woodbridge, July 20, 1816, " William Woodbridge Papers "
(MS, B. H. C.). " Peace is reported on the continent of Europe and if we get
peace also we shall make as much money as you want by the Indian trade."—
Astor to Crooks, February 14, 1814, " Ramsey Crooks Papers " (MS, B. H. C.).

[5] Astor to Crooks, October 28, 1813, " Crooks Papers." See also Astor to
Crooks, February 14, 25, 1814, Crooks to Astor, October 31, November 17,
December 1, 1813, May 8, 29, and June 19, 1814, " Crooks Papers."

[6] Williams to Boyd & Suydam, July 15, 1815, " John R. Williams Letterbook,
1815-1825 " (MS, in the possession of Frederick Douglas, Denver, Colorado).

[7] Williams to Boyd & Suydam, July 29, 1815, " Williams Letterbook."

[8] Williams to Boyd & Suydam, July 29, 1815, and March 9, 1816, Williams
to Henry Brevoort, May 31-June 1, 1816, " Williams Letterbook." The Custom
House in Detroit noted the arrival of piroques loaded with furs and peltries.—
United States Custom House, Detroit, " Daybook, 1815-1828 " (11 vols.; MS,
B. H. C.), June 5, 12, 1816.

[9] Williams to Brevoort, June 8, 1816, " Williams Letterbook."

[10] In 1815 Woodbridge, as Acting Governor of the territory, issued but three
licenses for the purpose of trading with the Indians. In 1816 nineteen traders
secured licenses.—" Record Book of Indian Trade Licenses, 1805-1817 " (MS,
B. H. C.), pp. 28-29.

[11] " An Act . . . to Regulate Trade and Intercourse with the Indian Tribes, and
to Preserve Peace on the Frontier," April 29, 1816. United States, *The Statutes
at Large of the United States . . . Concurrent Resolutions, Recent Treaties, Conventions, and Executive Proclamations* (55 vols.; Boston, 1845-1873, Washington,
1875-1942), III, 332-33. (Hereafter cited as *United States Statutes at Large.*)

[12] Kenneth Wiggins Porter, *John Jacob Astor, Business Man* (2 vols.; Cambridge,
1931), I, 164-65, 167-68.

[13] *Ibid.*, I, 253-55.

[14] Astor to Crooks, December 18, 1813, Robert Stuart to Crooks, March 21, 1815, " Crooks Papers."

[15] Porter, *op. cit.*, II, 699-700; *Detroit Gazette*, December 22, 1820.

[16] Macomb to the commanding officers of posts and detachments within the fifth military department (a letter introducing Ramsay Crooks), June 27, 1816, " Macomb Letterbook."

[17] *Detroit Gazette*, December 15, 22, 1820.

[18] *Ibid.*, December 15, 22, 1820; Williams to Boyd & Suydam, May 3, 1817, " Williams Letterbook "; Porter, *op. cit.*, II, 753-54.

[19] *Detroit Gazette*, December 15, 1820.

[20] Cincinnatus in *Ibid.*, November 21, 1817.

[21] *Ibid.*, June 1, 1821.

[22] Williams to Boyd & Suydam, May 3, 1817, November 18, 1820, " Williams Letterbook."

[23] Williams to Boyd & Suydam, November 10, 1821, February 24, 1822, " Williams Letterbook."

[24] Williams to Boyd & Suydam, September 12, 1821, Williams to Webb & Dummer, December 19, 1822, " Williams Letterbook."

[25] Williams to Boyd & Suydam, March 15, 1817, " Williams Letterbook."

[26] Williams to Webb & Dummer, May 13, 1820, Williams to David J. Boyd & Company, October 13, 1820, Williams to Boyd & Suydam, December 16, 1820, " Williams Letterbook."

[27] *Detroit Gazette*, December 22, 1820.

[28] David Thomas, *Travels Through the Western Country in the Summer of 1816* . . . (Auburn, N. Y., 1819), p. 314.

[29] *Detroit Gazette*, January 4, 1822.

[30] Williams to Boyd & Suydam, July 5, 1821, " Williams Letterbook." Two years later in a letter accompanying a shipment of furs Williams wrote: " Those furs having been caught in the Saginaw country and about Lake Huron are much superior to those caught in a more southern latitude and ought consequently to command a better price."—Williams to McHarg & King, June 28, 1823, " Williams Letterbook."

[31] Williams to Boyd & Suydam, May 15, July 10, 1817, Williams' memorandum, no date, summer, 1825, " Williams Letterbook." The fifty-five packs contained the following skins:

Deer	474	Otter	96	Cat	115
Raccoon	5,102	Fisher	70	Grey fox	74
Muskrat	7,912	Beaver	50 lb.	Red fox	6
Bear	76	Martin	108	Tiger	3
Cub	21	Mink	88		

[32] *Detroit Gazette*, August 19, 1819; Williams to Boyd & Storm, June 18, 1808, " Williams Papers "; Williams to Boyd & Suydam, December 30, 1815, " Williams Letterbook."

[33] Thomas, *op. cit.*, p. 315.

[34] Macomb to Major General Jacob Brown, July 27, 1816, " Macomb Letterbook."

[35] *Detroit Gazette*, January 29, 1819.

[36] *Ibid.*, January 29, August 13, 1819, and February 15, 1822. See also Thomas, *op. cit.*, pp. 314-15.

[37] *Detroit Gazette*, September 18, 1818.

[38] *Ibid.*, March 27, 1818.

[39] *Ibid.*, October 24, 1817.

[40] Witherell to his wife, October 14, 1815, "Benjamin Franklin Hawkins Witherell Papers" (MS, B. H. C.); *Niles' Weekly Register*, April 20, 1816; *Detroit Gazette*, July 25, 1817.

[41] *Detroit Gazette*, March 26, 1819.

[42] *Ibid.*, June 20, 1823.

[43] Elkanah Watson, *Men and Times of the Revolution or Memoirs of Elkanah Watson, Including Journals of Travels in Europe and America* . . . , Winslow C. Watson, ed. (New York, 1856), p. 430.

[44] Harrowby, *Detroit Gazette*, October 3, 1817.

[45] *Ibid.*, November 28, 1817.

[46] *Ibid.*, March 20, 1818.

[47] *Ibid.*, January 23, February 13, March 27, April 3, May 29, 1818.

[48] The prices of additional items were: lard, $20.00 a hundredweight, butter 31 cents a pound, cheese 25 cents, eggs 37 cents per dozen.—*Ibid.*, August 1, 1817. At times prices were even higher. See also United States House of Representatives, *House Document No. 60, 17th Congress, First Session* (Washington, 1822), pp. 115-16.

[49] *Detroit Gazette*, July 24, August 14, 1818.

[50] *Ibid.*, June 25, 1819.

[51] It added: "We . . . pay a *shilling* a *pound* for *poor* mutton, eight and ten cents a pound for *poor* beef—$20 to $25, per bbl. for ordinary pork, and for every eatable a price in like proportion."—*Ibid.*, September 17, 1819. Prices evidently were at their height during the winter months.—*Ibid.*, January 22, April 30, 1819.

[52] Quoted in *ibid.*, October 8, 1819.

[53] *Ibid.*, November 16, 23, 1819.

[54] Williams to [James McCloskey], July 31, 1822, "Williams Papers." A subsequent passage in this letter is of interest in that it discloses the opinions of a native son in regard to the advisability of migrating to Michigan—much as he wished to see the country settled: "What a strange infatuation for men that are well off and well-settled in a far wealthier country than ours, with every advantage resulting from good schools and other improvements in relation to comforts and conveniences, to desire to change their fine houses, well improved farms, and wholesome laws for wilds—mosquitoes—trouble—labor and an indifferent government—but they must know their own business. I have not *one* word to say to deter them from carrying their plans into execution."

[55] *Detroit Gazette*, May 11, 1821. See also issues for January 22, and July 30, 1819.

[56] *Ibid.*, June 14, 1822.

[57] *Ibid.*, May 11, August 10, October 19, 1821, January 25, March 22, May 31, 1822.

[58] *Ibid.*, June 14, 1822.

[59] *Ibid.*, August 22, December 27, 1822. The editor of the *Gazette* took particular notice of exceptional vegetables grown in other regions, and countered with descriptions of even greater feats in Michigan.—*Ibid.*, September 8, 1820, October 26, December 7, 1821, November 22, 1822, and October 18, 1825.

[60] *Ibid.*, February 28, May 23, June 13, and December 26, 1823.

[61] *Ibid.*, April 9, 1824.

[62] *Ibid.*, June 28, 1825.

[63] *Ibid.*, December 13, 1825.

[64] *Ibid.*, July 25, September 19, October 3, and November 7, 1817. Darby, visiting Detroit in 1818, noted that the fruit trees were " remarkably productive."— William Darby, *A Tour from the City of New York to Detroit in the Michigan Territory, Made Between the 2nd of May and the 22nd of September, 1818* (New York, 1819), p. 200.

[65] Cider was valued at from $4.50 to $7.00 per barrel, although it was reported to have sold for $11.00 per barrel in the summer of 1817. Between April 1, 1817 and March 31, 1818, 536 barrels of cider and 230 barrels of apples were exported from Detroit to domestic markets; for the entire year, 1818, 753 barrels of cider and 653 barrels of apples were exported.—Thomas, *op. cit.*, p. 314; *Detroit Gazette*, September 19, 1817, January 29, 1819.

[66] *Detroit Gazette*, November 5, 1819.

[67] *Ibid.*, January 19, 1821.

[68] Early in 1826 an observer declared that the French farmers " appear reconciled to let the earth rest and the houses go to decay around them; and the orchards to decline and die."—Thomas Lorraine McKenney, *Sketches of a Tour to the Lakes, of the Character and Customs of the Chippeway Indians, and of Incidents Connected with the Treaty of Fond du Lac* (Baltimore, 1827), p. 126. See also Bela Hubbard, *Memorials of a Half-Century* (New York and London, 1888), pp. 125-27.

[69] Cass to the Secretary of War, May 31, 1816, Carter, *op. cit.*, X, 642-43; David Abbott to Woodbridge, April 2, 1816, " Woodbridge Papers."

[70] Macomb to Crawford, August 17, 1816, " Macomb Letterbook."

[71] *Detroit Gazette*, July 25, 1817. For the year ending March 31, 1818, there arrived at Detroit: 273 barrels of beef, valued at $25.00 per barrel; 683 barrels of pork, valued at $25.00 per barrel; 423 firkins (a firkin was equivalent to one-fourth of a barrel, or 56 pounds) of butter, valued at $9.00 per firkin; 373 firkins of lard, valued at $8.00 per firkin.—Thomas, *op. cit.*, pp. 314-15. For the entire year 1818 there was shipped to Detroit: 888 barrels of pork, 10 barrels of beef, and 693 firkins of butter. In addition there arrived by land " 1,042 beef cattle and 1,435 fat hogs." A minor portion of these imports was reshipped to other posts in the territory.—*Detroit Gazette*, January 29, 1819.

[72] *Detroit Gazette*, May 17, 1825.

[73] *Ibid.*, November 1, 1825; Hubbard, *op. cit.*, pp. 141-42.

[74] In 1816 David Thomas noted that whitefish brought from Detroit were for sale in Vincennes, Indiana. They were probably sent there by Ohio fisherman.— Thomas, *op. cit.*, p. 195. During the year ending March 31, 1818, 870 barrels of fish, valued at $10.00 per barrel, were exported from Detroit.—*Ibid.*, p. 314. See also the *Detroit Gazette*, November 14, 1817.

[75] *Detroit Gazette*, November 14, 1817. See also the issue of March 27, 1818.

[76] Salt sold for $7.00 per barrel in Detroit at this time.—" F. T. & J. Palmer, Daybook, July 20, 1818-March 13, 1819 " (MS, B. H. C.), August 26, 1818. In 1819 the territory passed a law regulating the packing of fish, and an inspector was appointed to examine them. It was required that one-half bushel of salt be used in each barrel.—*Detroit Gazette*, October 22, 29, 1819.

[77] *Detroit Gazette*, December 29, 1820. A contributor to the *Gazette* pointed out that because of the shortness of the fishing season and the fact that it arrived in

the fall of the year, citizens could engage in the industry without injury to agricultural pursuits. He also noted that fish oil might become a valuable by-product of the industry.—*Ibid.*, January 12, 1821.

[78] *Ibid.*, October 26, 1821, October 10, 1823, and November 12, 1824.

[79] *Ibid.*, November 22, 1822. The increase in value over 1818 was much more substantial than it appears, for by 1822 the dollar had greatly appreciated.

[80] *Ibid.*, October 10, 1823.

[81] *Ibid.*, November 7, 28, 1823.

[82] *Ibid.*, October 29, November 12, 1824.

[83] *Ibid.*, July 12, 1825; Michigan, *Laws of the Territory of Michigan* (4 vols.; Lansing, 1871-1884), II, 286.

[84] *Detroit Gazette*, June 21, 1822; Williams to John C. Devereux, November 3, 1823, " Williams Letterbook."

[85] *Detroit Gazette*, November 1, 1825.

[86] *Ibid.*, October 25, November 8, 1825.

[87] " The white fish of the lakes promise to become, indeed now are, a valuable article for export from Detroit. They are worth six or seven dollars a barrel."—*Niles' Weekly Register*, January 14, 1826. Hubbard's claim that the first exportation of whitefish from Detroit occurred in 1825 is obviously in error.—Hubbard, *op. cit.*, p. 275.

[88] *Detroit Gazette*, January 7, 1820; Henry Rowe Schoolcraft, *Narrative Journal of Travels . . . from Detroit through the Great Chain of American Lakes to the Sources of the Mississippi River . . . in the Year 1820* (Albany, 1821), p. 65.

[89] The extent of this trade with New York, plus the fact that the majority of the newcomers to Michigan were from that state, led the *Gazette* to remark: " Our business and intercourse, natural and habitual, is with *New York*, and we are in fact, except in a political point of view, an extended part of that state."—*Detroit Gazette*, January 4, 1822. See also the issues of April 10, 1818 and August 13, 1819; George C. Bates, " The By-Gone Merchants," *Michigan Pioneer and Historical Society, Collections*, XXII, 369-70; Williams to Boyd & Suydam, January 23, 1818, September 12, 1821, " Williams Letterbook."

[90] Most of the local merchants advertised their wares regularly in the columns of the *Detroit Gazette*, their advertisements bearing testimony to the wide assortment of merchandise they carried in stock.—*Detroit Gazette*, 1817-25, *passim*.

[91] *House Document No. 60*, pp. 109-11.

[92] Cass claimed that in 1816 the average daily number of Indians in Detroit was 400.—*Ibid.*, p. 110. *Detroit Gazette*, November 21, 1823, July 30, 1824.

[93] A few of the larger expenditures for contingencies were: $273.73 for goods purchased from Henry J. Hunt; $191.64, from Mack & Conant; and $151.67, from T. S. Wendell. Following is an itemized account of this last expenditure: " For 10 flat files, at 7 s., 12 half round, do., at 6 s., 450 lbs. iron at 1 s. 2 d., one grindstone, 148 lbs. [at] $3\frac{1}{2}$ cts. [per lb.], two spades, at 12 s., 10 yds. wire, [at] 6 cts., two lbs. nails, at 1 s. 6 d., one lb. borax, 20 s., 10 files, at 3 s. 6 d., 2 rattail do. at 2 s. 6 d., 72 lbs. German steel, at 3 s. 6 d., 54 $\frac{1}{4}$ E. B. steel at 2 s. 6 d., one grass scythe, at 9 s., six files half round, at 6 s., 200 quills at 6 s., two quires folio post at 6 s., three do. foolscap, at 3 s., one fur hat at 36 s."—*House Document No. 60.*, pp. 84-87.

[94] Supplies and trade goods purchased of Abraham Edwards totalled $859.10, Hunt, 765.58\frac{1}{4}$, Mack & Conant, 306.56\frac{1}{4}$, D. G. Jones, $107.33, and Chauncey S. Payne, $1,402.51. Itemized, this last purchase was for the following: " For

85 gorgets, $152.91; 41 pair arm bands, $357.19; 336 broaches, 4 sizes, $403.13; 103 ear wheels, $152.50; 3,800 small broaches, 218 dolls; 33 pair ear bobs, 36 dolls.; 33 pr. wrist bands, $82.78."—*Ibid.*, pp. 88-93.

[95] *Ibid.*, pp. 93-100. See also Williams to Boyd & Suydam, September 12, 1821, " Williams Letterbook."

[96] Williams noted that persons residing at a distance from Detroit contributed much to the business of the city. He claimed that they came from as far as the Miami Bay region, the Thames River (Canada), the shores of the St. Clair River, as well as from the interior of the territory.—Williams to A. S. Griswold, February 28, 1825, " Williams Letterbook." See also *Detroit Gazette*, January 2, 1824.

[97] *Detroit Gazette*, 1824-25, *passim.*

[98] The following advertisement illustrates the wide variety of merchandise which Abbott offered for sale: " The subscriber has on hand, and will sell the same *very low for cash,* the following articles, viz., 200 pairs Blankets assorted, 10 pieces Flannels, 6 pieces Bombazetts, 100 barrels Salt, 50 barrels Whiskey, 10 barrels Maple Sugar, 3 barrels Pitch, 50 boxes cut Nails, 3 barrels and 2 kegs Hogs-Lard, and seventeen thousand feet boards. Also ten boxes domestic goods, consisting of Cotton Shirtings, Sheetings, Tickings, and Factory Stripes."—*Ibid.*, June 19, 1818. In 1815 Solomon Sibley sold Ohio produce at a commission rate of 5 per cent.— Darius Henderson to Sibley, March 22, 1815, Sibley to Henderson, May 22, 1815, " Solomon Sibley Papers " (MS, B. H. C.). See also Williams to Captain Jedediah Rogers, April 1, 1820, Williams to William James, August 6, 1825, " Williams Letterbook."

[99] Williams to E. Mather & Co., January 19, 1825, Williams to A. S. Griswold, February 28, 1825, " Williams Letterbook."

[100] *Detroit Gazette*, May 10, 1825.

[101] *Ibid.*, May 10, 31, June 28, 1825. The firm of Dorr & Brewster, which took over a " large and commodious warehouse " in the fall of 1825 and began operations in the forwarding and commission business, advertised: " Advances will be made on property consigned to them to sell, and the utmost pains taken to render satisfaction."—*Ibid.*, September 27, 1825.

[102] See advertisements of such firms as R. & O. Johnson, F. & T. Palmer, and Shubael Conant & Co. in *Detroit Gazette*, July 25, December 12, 1817, and April 24, 1818. See also Williams to Rufus Brown, May 16, 1818, " Williams Letterbook."

[103] *Detroit Gazette*, November 21, 1817.

[104] *Ibid.*, December 19, 1817.

[105] *Ibid.*, October 8, 1819.

[106] *Ibid.*, July 13, 1821.

[107] *Ibid.*, February 22, 1822.

[108] *Ibid.*, January 9, 1824. F. P. Browning, who began business a few months later, called his establishment, the " Detroit Cash & Barter Store."—*Ibid.*, October 8, 1824.

[109] *Ibid.*, August 2, 1822. Honey was priced at ten cents and beeswax at twenty-six cents a pound in 1823.—*Ibid.*, February 28, 1823.

[110] Maple sugar sold for five cents a pound.—*Ibid.*, February 28, 1823, February 28, 1824, and September 20, 1825.

[111] One merchant advertised: " The subscriber will pay three dollars per cwt. for good black salts of lye, half cash and half goods, delivered at his ashery—also 15 cents per bushel in goods, for good house ashes, and 8 cents per bushel for

good field ashes, delivered at his ashery—the highest price paid for pot and pearl ashes."—*Ibid.*, January 30, 1824. In 1825 Williams wrote to a New York associate: " I have been making enquiries relating to ashes—There is a person from the country who has or will have by the opening of navigation, twenty or thirty tons of potash for which he asks $100 per ton at this place—If you wish me to purchase on your acct. advise me of your determination in that respect as soon as practicable—as I have promised to give him an answer soon. . . . According to appearances as the country is settling fast there will be considerable quantity of ashes exported from this place soon and the quantity must annually increase with the growth of the settlements."—Williams to William & John James, January 20, 1825. " Williams Letterbook."

[112] *Detroit Gazette*, July 30, 1819.

[113] Cass to Crawford, May 31, 1816, Carter, *op. cit.*, X, 642.

[114] *Detroit Gazette*, May 11, 1821.

[115] The proprietors added that " their mill is in good order, and they feel confident of being able to give satisfaction to all who may send their cloth to them. Their terms for dressing cloth will be found to be very reasonable—not differeng from those of clothiers in the state of New York."—*Ibid.*, November 7, 1823.

[116] The *Gazette* claimed that wool was sent 1,080 miles " going and coming " to be carded at this establishment.—*Ibid.*, October 8, 1824.

[117] " The country around Detroit is uncommonly flat and in none of the rivers is there a fall sufficient to turn even a gristmill."—Isaac Weld, Jr., *Travels through the States of North America and the Provinces of Upper Canada during the Years 1795, 1796, and 1797* (London, 1799), p. 354.

[118] When coal deposits were discovered along the Lake Huron shore of the peninsula in 1825, the *Gazette* predicted: " Should this article be found in such quantities as to justify the establishment of mining operations in that quarter, Detroit would soon become a manufacturing town. We are told that steam power, when *coal* is used as fuel, is nearly as cheap as water power, in propelling machinery."—*Detroit Gazette*, September 13, 1825.

[119] *Ibid.*, August 10, 1821; Hubbard, *op. cit.*, p. 135.

[120] Substantial amounts of lumber were imported from the River Thames district of Canada, even though a duty of 25 to 30 per cent was charged. " Leonard Westbrook imported from R. Thames, U.C. [Upper Canada] a Raft of Boards—15,934 ft. price 10 per thousand—duties paid—39.93."—United States Custom House, Detroit, " Daybook, 1815-1828 " (11 vols.; MS, B. H. C.), June 14, 1815. Eight thousand feet of boards and 16,000 shingles, valued at $224.00 were imported from Dorchester, U.C. in 1816.—*Ibid.*, July 19, 1816. See also United States Custom House, Detroit, " Impost Book, 1815-1823 " (MS, B. H. C.), pp. 11, 13, 14. During the summer of 1817, boards sold for $25.00 per M.; planking, $40.00 per M.; shingles, $4.00 per M.; and lath, $5.00 per M.—*Detroit Gazette*, August 1, 1817. The prices for 1823 were: boards, pine, $8.00 to $12.50 per M.; oak, $12.50 per M.; shingles, $1.75 per M.; scantling, $9.00 per M.; lath, $10.00 per M.; square timber, eight cents per foot. (In comparing these prices it must be remembered that during the interim there had been an appreciation of the currency.)—*Ibid.*, February 28, 1823. See also Estwick Evans, " Evans' Pedestrious Tour of Four Thousand Miles—1818," in Reuben Gold Thwaites, *Early Western Travels, 1748-1846* . . . (32 vols.; Cleveland, 1904), p. 220. Lumber was a scarce commodity in Detroit as late as 1825. The editor of the *Herald* wrote: " It is worthy of remark, that at this season of the year, there is not a thousand feet of lumber to be purchased in Detroit, that article, which could have been bought in the month of June at $10.00 per M. has now risen to $15.00 per M. and is not to be had at that price."—*Michigan Herald*, October 18, 1825.

[121] *Detroit Gazette*, April 3, 1818, November 5, 1819. Conner's mill was destroyed by fire in 1823.—*Ibid.*, November 28, 1823.

[122] *Ibid.*, July 6, August 10, 1821.

[123] *Ibid.*, September 20, 1825.

[124] *Ibid.*, July 26, 1825.

[125] *Ibid.*, February 11, 1820.

[126] *Ibid.*, August 10, 1821.

[127] It is difficult to obtain any clear conception of the extent of manufactures at this time. Information obtained during the taking of the fourth census in 1820 is incomplete and is compiled by counties. Since Detroit was the only settled place of importance in Wayne County at the time, the statistics for the county were in all probability closely aligned to those of the city. They indicate that the eleven manufacturing establishments employed thirty-one men and three boys and girls. Products included coopers wares, flour and meal, hats, leather, lumber, saddles, etc., tin ware, and whiskey.—*American State Papers* (38 vols.; Washington, 1832-61), *Finance*, IV, 221. For a more detailed analysis of this information, see Almon Ernest Parkins, *The Historical Geography of Detroit* (Lansing, 1918), pp. 282-83.

[128] Evans, *op. cit.*, p. 220.

[129] *Detroit Gazette*, January 29, 1819.

[130] *Ibid.*, April 25, 1819.

[131] *Ibid.*, January 29, 1819.

[132] *Ibid.*, September 17, 1819.

[133] Cass to the Secretary of War, June 6, 1816, Carter, *op. cit.*, X, 649. Detailed accounts of the expenditures of the Indian Department at Detroit may be found in *House Document No. 60*, pp. 74-108, *passim.*

[134] By 1821 there were located in Pontiac "1 tanner and currier, 1 shoemaker, 1 blacksmith, 1 cabinetmaker, 1 wheelwright, 3 carpenters, and 1 brickmaker."—*Detroit Gazette*, February 2, 1821. See also Parkins, *op. cit.*, 283-85.

[135] At the close of 1818 the buildings in Detroit numbered 273, of which 142 were private dwellings. By 1824 the city contained 366 buildings, private homes numbering 155.—*Detroit Gazette*, January 29, 1819, January 2, 1824.

[136] *Ibid.*, January 2, 1824.

[137] The *Gazette* declared October 12, 1821: "Much inconvenience has been sustained by the citizens of Detroit for the want of a few good and industrious brickmakers."

[138] Of these, two-story buildings numbered twenty-two, story-and-a-half buildings, seventeen, and one-story buildings, nineteen.—Clarence M. Burton, *History of Detroit, 1780-1850, Financial and Commercial* (Detroit, 1917), p. 94. See also *Michigan Herald*, October 4, 1825.

[139] *Ibid.*, October 4, 1825.

[140] In order to promote the production of barley, Abbott offered a premium of $20.00 for the best 100 bushels raised in Michigan during the year, and $10.00 for the second best. He offered to pay "three shillings and six pence per bushel, in cash," for barley delivered at the brewery.—*Detroit Gazette*, February 28, 1823, December 31, 1824.

[141] He also advertised that "all kinds of turning, of wood and iron, will be done."—*Ibid.*, December 19, 1823.

[142] *Ibid.*, June 18, 1824.

[143] *Ibid.*, December 6, 1825.

CHAPTER VI

Detroit at the Close of 1825

In the fall of 1825 as the roar of cannon echoing back and forth across the state of New York heralded the completion of the Erie Canal and the first canal boat began its eastward journey toward tidewater, a new era dawned for Detroit. During the next decade a swelling tide of westward migration was to course through this man-made channel and surge on into the sparsely settled lands of northern Ohio and southern Michigan. Detroit, on the direct line of this great movement, was to become the *entrepot* of a vast and fertile region, peopled by an energetic and ambitious husbandry.

As the year 1825 drew to a close, the citizens of Detroit could look with confidence to the future of their city, for the signs seemed to indicate that it would soon occupy a dominant position in the economy of the lake region. Its prospects were particularly gratifying to those residents who had witnessed the developments of the previous ten years. In moments of reverie their thoughts probably returned to the unhappy months in 1815 and 1816 when the stricken frontier city depended upon federal gratuities to feed its starving and a small number of open boats and sailing vessels furnished an undependable means of communication with the

rest of the nation. They recalled the enthusiasm of the populace
when the first road was projected through the wilderness toward
the Ohio settlements and the jubilation occasioned by the arrival
of the *Walk-in-the-Water*. As they watched the steamboats and
sailing vessels deposit their human cargoes in ever-increasing numbers, they were reminded of the time a few years before when
the public lands in the territory were first placed on the market
and a few hardy citizens ventured into the wild hinterland to
blaze the way for the thousands that were to follow. They remem-
bered that July day in 1817 when the *Detroit Gazette* first made is
appearance and recalled its staunch endeavors in subsequent years
to promote the welfare of Detroit and Michigan Territory. As
they completed business transactions with money of certain value,
their thoughts reverted to that dark period in 1819 when the
well-secured bills of the Bank of Michigan first began to circulate
in the city, offering relief to a populace harassed by questionable
currency. They regarded with interest the ambitious " Yankees "
whose activity and enterprise had pervaded the city and trans-
formed it into a vigorous American community. They could
contemplate with satisfaction the manifold accomplishments of
the decade. Indeed, they had witnessed the deliverance of Detroit
from many of the economic bonds which had thwarted its development for more than a century, and, could they have but known,
they had seen the foundations laid for the great metropolis of
the future.

Visiting Detroit in the spring of 1826, a learned traveler surveyed its situation and that of the surrounding region, and
observed:

> The shores on the British side are bolder than those on the
> American, but look as they must have looked half a century
> ago. There appears to be nothing going on in the way of
> improvement, either in lands or buildings; but a new face

is put on things on the American side, save where, here and there, an old French family lingers, and wherever that is, the picture of inactivity and barrenness is visible, just as if reflected from the Canada shores.[1]

CHAPTER VI—Notes

[1] Thomas Lorraine McKenney, *Sketches of a Tour to the Lakes, of the Character and Customs of the Chippeway Indians, and of Incidents connected with the Treaty of Fond du Lac* (Baltimore, 1827), p. 109.

Bibliography

PRIMARY

I. Unpublished

Brady, Joriah. "Papers." MS, Burton Historical Collection, Detroit Public Library.

Cass, Lewis. "Papers." MS, Burton Historical Collection, Detroit Public Library.

Catlin, George B. "Digest of the Act of Incorporation of the Town of Detroit on October 24, 1815 and also a Digest of the Proceedings of the Board of Trustees Adopted by the Board of the Governor & Judges of the Northwest Territory to September 6, 1824." Typescript, Burton Historical Collection, Detroit Public Library.

Crooks, Ramsay. "Papers." MS, Burton Historical Collection, Detroit Public Library.

Fraser, Alexander David. "Papers." MS, Burton Historical Collection, Detroit Public Library.

Larned, Charles. "Papers." MS, Burton Historical Collection, Detroit Public Library.

McArthur, Duncan. "Papers." MS and photostats, Burton Historical Collection, Detroit Public Library.

Macomb, Alexander. "Letterbook, 1807-1819." Typescript, Burton Historical Collection, Detroit Public Library.

Palmer, F. T. & J. "Daybook, July 20, 1818-March 13, 1819." MS, Burton Historical Collection, Detroit Public Library.

Palmer, Thomas. "Papers." MS, Burton Historical Collection, Detroit Public Library.

"Record Book of Indian Trade Licenses, 1805-1817." MS, Burton Historical Collection, Detroit Public Library.

Richard, Gabriel. "Papers." MS, Burton Historical Collection, Detroit Public Library.

Sibley, Solomon. "Papers." MS, Burton Historical Collection, Detroit Public Library.

United States Custom House, Detroit, William Woodbridge, Collector. "Daybook, 1815-1828." 11 vols.; MS, Burton Historical Collection, Detroit Public Library.

———. "Impost Book, 1815-1823." MS, Burton Historical Collection, Detroit Public Library.

———. "Vessel Register, 1815-1824." MS, Burton Historical Collection, Detroit Public Library.

Williams, John R. "Letterbook, 1815-1825." MS in the possession of Frederick Douglas, Denver, Colorado.

———. "Papers." MS, Burton Historical Collection, Detroit Public Library.

Witherell, Benjamin Franklin Hawkins. "Papers." MS, Burton Historical Collection, Detroit Public Library.

Woodbridge, William. "Papers." MS, Burton Historical Collection, Detroit Public Library.

Woodward, Augustus Brevoort. "Papers." MS, Burton Historical Collection, Detroit Public Library.

II. BOOKS AND HISTORICAL COLLECTIONS

Birkbeck, Morris. *Notes on a Journey in America, from the Coast of Virginia to the Territory of Illinois.* London: printed by Severn & Radington for Ridgway and Sons, 1818.

Blowe, Daniel. *A Geographical, Commercial, and Agricultural View of the United States of America, Forming a Complete Emigrant's Directory throughout Every Part of the Republic Particularly the Western States and Territories.* Liverpool: H. Fisher, 1819.

Brown, Samuel R. *Views on Lake Erie.* Troy, New York: printed by Francis Adamcourt, 1814.

Buttrick, Tilly, Jr. "Buttrick's Voyages, Travels, and Discoveries, 1812-1819." In Reuben Gold Thwaites, *Early Western Travels, 1748-1846,* VIII, 15-89.

Darby, William. *A Tour from the City of New York, to Detroit, in the Michigan Territory, Made between the 2nd of May and the 22nd of September, 1818.* New York: Kirk and Mercein, 1819.

Evans, Estwick. "Evans' Pedestrious Tour of Four Thousand Miles—1818." In Reuben Gold Thwaites, *Early Western Travels, 1748-1846,* VIII, 91-364.

Fearon, Henry Bradshaw. *Sketches of America. A Narrative of a Journey of Five Thousand Miles through the Eastern and Western States of America.* 3rd ed.; London: Longman, Hurst, Rees, Orme, and Brown, 1819.

Flint, James. "Letters from America, 1818 to 1820." In Reuben Gold Thwaites, *Early Western Travels, 1748-1846,* IX.

McKenney, Thomas Lorraine. *Sketches of a Tour to the Lakes, of the Character and Customs of the Chippeway Indians, and of Incidents Connected with the Treaty of Fond du Lac.* Baltimore: Fielding Lucas, Jr., 1827.

Michigan Pioneer and Historical Society, Collections. 40 vols.; Lansing, Michigan: [Michigan Pioneer and Historical Society], 1877-1912; Michigan Historical Commission, 1915-1929.

Schoolcraft, Henry Rowe. *Narrative Journal of Travels through the Northwestern Regions of the United States; Extending from Detroit through the Great Chain of American Lakes, to the Sources of the Mississippi River. Performed as a Member of the Expedition under Governor Cass in the Year 1820.* Albany: E. & E. Hosford, 1821.

―――――. *Personal Memoirs of a Residence of Thirty Years with the Indian Tribes on the American Frontiers with Brief Notices of Passing Events, Facts, and Opinions, A. D. 1812 to A. D. 1842.* Philadelphia: Lippincott, Grambo and Co., 1851.

―――――. *Travels in the Central Portions of the Mississippi Valley: Comprising Observations on Its Mineral Geography, Internal Resources, and Aboriginal Population. (Performed Under the Sanction of Government, in the Year 1821).* New York: Collins and Hannay, 1825.

Schultz, Christian. *Travels on an Inland Voyage through the States of New York, Pennsylvania, Virginia, Ohio, Kentucky and Tennessee, and the Territories of Indiana, Louisiana, Mississippi, and New Orleans. Performed in the Years 1807 and 1808. Including a Tour of Nearly Six Thousand Miles. With Maps and Plates.* 2 vols.; New York; printed by Isaac Riley, 1810.

Spafford, Horatio G. *A Pocket Guide for Tourist and Traveler along the Line of the Canals, and the Interior Commerce of the State of New York.* 2nd ed., with additions and corrections; Troy, New York: W. S. Parker, 1825.

Thomas, David. *Travels through the Western Country in the Summer of 1816. Including Notices of the Natural History, Antiquities, Topography, Agriculture, Commerce, and Manufacturing; with a Map of the Wabash Country, Now Settling.* Auburn, New York: printed by David Rumsey, 1819.

Thwaites, Reuben Gold. *Early Western Travels, 1748-1846. A Series of Annotated Reprints of Some of the Best and Rarest Contemporary Volumes of Travel, Descriptive of the Aborigines and Social and Economic Conditions in the Middle and Far West, During the Period of Early American Settlement.* 32 vols.; Cleveland: Arthur H. Clark Co., 1904.

Volney, C. F. *A View of the Soil and Climate of the United States of America: With Supplementary Remarks upon Florida;*

on the Aboriginal Tribes of America. Translated, with occasional remarks by C. B. Brown. Philadelphia: J. Conrad & Co., 1804.

Watson, Elkanah. *Men and Times of the Revolution; or, Memoirs of Elkanah Watson, Including Journals of Travels in Europe and America from 1777 to 1842, with His Correspondence with Public Men and Reminiscences and Incidents of the Revolution.* Winslow C. Watson, ed. New York: Dana and Company, 1856.

Weld, Jr., Isaac. *Travels through the States of North America and the Provinces of Upper Canada during the Years 1795, 1796, and 1797.* London: J. Stockdale, 1799.

III. NEWSPAPERS AND PERIODICALS

Detroit Gazette. 1817-1826.
Michigan Herald. Detroit, 1825-1826.
Niagara Patriot. Buffalo, New York. September 15, 1818.
Niles' Weekly Register. Baltimore, Maryland, Vols. 1-30. 1812-1826.

IV. OFFICIAL DOCUMENTS

American State Papers. Documents, Legislative and Executive, of the Congress of the United States . . . Selected and Edited under the Authority of Congress. . . . 38 vols.; Washington: Gales and Seaton, 1832-61.

Burton, Clarence M., comp., and M. Agnes Burton, ed., *Governor and Judges Journal Proceedings of the Land Board of Detroit.* [Detroit]: n. pub., 1915.

Carter, Clarence Edwin, ed. and comp. *The Territorial Papers of the United States.* 10 vols.; Washington: Government Printing Office, 1934-1942.

Michigan. *Laws of the Territory of Michigan.* 4 vols.; Lansing: W. S. George & Co., 1871-1884.

Richardson, James D., comp. *A Compilation of the Messages and Papers of the Presidents.* Rev. ed., 11 vols.; n. p.: Bureau of National Literature and Art, 1913.

United States. *Fifth Census: or, Enumeration of the Inhabitants of the United States, 1830, to Which is Prefixed a Schedule of the Whole Number of Persons within the Several Districts of the United States. Taken According to the Acts of 1790, 1800, 1810, 1820.* Washington: Duff Green, 1832.

———. *The Statutes at Large of the United States . . . Concurrent Resolutions, Recent Treaties, Conventions and Executive Proclamations.* 55 vols.; Boston: Charles C. Little and James Brown, 1845-1873 (vols. 1-17) ; Washington: Government Printing Office, 1875-1942 (vols. 18-55).

————. *Treaties and Conventions Concluded between the United States of America and Other Powers Since July 4, 1776; Containing Notes, with Reference to Negotiations Preceding the Several Treaties, to the Executive, Legislative, or Judicial Construction of Them, and to the Causes of the Abrogation of Some of Them; a Chronological List of Treaties and an Analytical Index.* Washington: Government Printing Office, 1889.

United States House of Representatives. *Letter from the Secretary of War, Transmitting (in Obedience to a Resolution of the House of Representatives of the 18th Ult.) Information in Relation to the Superintendency of Indian Affairs in the Territory of Michigan during the Year 1820, and Part of the Year 1821. House Document No. 60, 17th Congress, 1st Session.* Washington: Gales & Seaton, 1822.

————. *Message from the President of the United States, Transmitting Pursuant to a Resolution of the House of Representatives of Ninth Dec. Last, Information of the Roads Made or in Progress, under Authority of the Executive of the United States; the States and Territories through Which They Pass, or are Intended to Pass; the Periods when They Were Ordered to be Made, and How Far They have been Executed. House Document No. 61. 15th Congress, 1st Session.* Washington: E. DeKrafft, 1818.

————. *Military Road in Michigan. House Report No. 42, 19th Congress, 1st Session.* [Washington (?)]: [Gales & Seaton (?)], [1826 (?)].

SECONDARY

I. UNPUBLISHED

Catlin, George B. "Papers." MS, Burton Historical Collection, Detroit Public Library.

II. BOOKS AND PAMPHLETS

[Albany Argus (?)]. *Outlines of the Life and Character of General Lewis Cass.* Albany: Joel Munsell, printer, 1848.

Burton, Clarence M. *History of Detroit, 1780-1850. Financial and Commercial.* Report of the Historiographer. Detroit: n. pub., 1917.

————. *The City of Detroit, Michigan, 1701-1922.* 5 vols. Detroit: S. J. Clarke Publishing Co., 1922.

Cass, Lewis, Henry R. Schoolcraft, Henry Whiting, and John Biddle. *Historical and Scientific Sketches of Michigan, Comprising a Series of Discourses Delivered before the Historical Society of Michigan, and Other Interesting Papers Relative to the Territory.* Detroit: S. Wells and G. L. Whitney, 1834.

Dewey, Davis Rich. *Financial History of the United States.* 12th ed.; New York, London, and Toronto: Longmans, Green and Co., 1934.

Donaldson, Thomas. *The Public Domain. Its History, with Statistics, with References to the National Domain, Colonization, Acquirement of Territory, the Survey, Administration and Several Methods of Sale and Disposition of the Public Domain of the United States, with Sketch of Legislative History of the Land States and Territories, and References to the Land System of the Colonies, and also that of Several Foreign Governments.* Washington: Government Printing Office, 1884.

[Durant, Samuel W.] *History of Oakland County, Michigan. With Illustrations Descriptive of Its Scenery, Palatial Residences, Public Buildings, Fine Blocks, and Important Manufactories, from Original Sketches by Artists of the Highest Ability.* Philadelphia: L. H. Everts & Co., 1877.

Farmer, Silas. *The History of Detroit and Michigan; or, the Metropolis Illustrated; a Chronological Cyclopaedia of the Past and Present, Including a Full Record of Territorial Days in Michigan, and the Annals of Wayne County.* Detroit: Silas Farmer & Co., 1884.

Fuller, George Newman. *Economic and Social Beginnings of Michigan. A Study of the Settlement of the Lower Peninsula During the Territorial Period, 1805-1837.* Lansing: [Michigan Historical Commission], 1916.

Gouge, William M. *A Short History of Paper Money and Banking in the United States, Including an Account of Provincial and Continental Paper Money. To Which is Prefixed, An Inquiry into the Principles of the System.* Philadelphia; printed by T. W. Ustick, 1833.

[Hildreth, Richard]. *The History of Banks: to Which is Added, a Demonstration of the Advantages and Necessity of Free Competition in the Business of Banking.* Boston: Hilliard, Gray, & Co., 1837.

Hubbard, Bela. *Memorials of a Half-Century in Michigan and the Lake Region.* New York and London: G. P. Putnam's Sons, 1888.

Hulbert, Archer Butler. *Historic Highways of America.* 16 vols.; Cleveland: A. H. Clark Co., 1902-1905.

Kingsford, William. *The History of Canada.* 10 vols.; Toronto: Roswell & Hutchinson, 1887-1898.

MacCabe, Julius P. Bolivar. *Directory of the City of Detroit with Its Environs and Register of Michigan for the Year 1837.* Detroit: printed by William Harsha, 1837.

[Mansfield, John Brandt]. *History of the Great Lakes.* 2 vols.; Chicago: J. H. Beers & Co., 1899.

Mills, James Cooke. *Our Inland Seas. Their Shipping & Commerce for Three Centuries.* Chicago: A. C. McClurg & Co., 1910.

Morrison, John Harrison. *History of American Steam Navigation.* New York: W. F. Sametz & Co., Inc., 1903.

Parkins, Almon Ernest. *The Historical Geography of Detroit.* Lansing: Michigan Historical Commission, 1918.

Pierce, Bessie Louise. *A History of Chicago.* 2 vols.; New York and London: A. A. Knopf, 1937-1940.

Plumb, Ralph G. *History of the Navigation of the Great Lakes.* Washington: Government Printing Office, 1911.

Porter, Kenneth Wiggins. *John Jacob Astor, Business Man.* 2 vols.; Cambridge: Harvard University Press, 1931.

Weisenburger, Francis P. *The Passing of the Frontier, 1825-1850.* Vol. III of *The History of the State of Ohio.* Carl Wittke, ed. Columbus: Ohio State Archaeological and Historical Society, 1941.

III. ARTICLES

Bates, George C. "The By-gone Merchants." *Michigan Pioneer and Historical Society, Collections,* XXII (1894), 369-389.

Bird, Colonel William A. "New York State, Early Transportation." *Buffalo Historical Society, Publications.* II (1880), 17-32.

Bliss, A. N. "Federal Land Grants for Internal Improvements." *Michigan Pioneer and Historical Society, Collections,* VII (1884), 52-68.

Campbell, James V. "Sketches of Charles C. Trowbridge." *Michigan Pioneer and Historical Society, Collections,* VI (1883), 478-491.

Clarkson, D. "Pioneer Sketches." *Michigan Pioneer and Historical Society, Collections,* I (1874-76), 509-510.

Drake, Thomas J. "History of Oakland County." *Michigan Pioneer and Historical Society, Collections,* III (1881), 559-572.

Felch, Alpheus. "The Indians of Michigan and the Cession of their Lands to the United States by Treaties." *Michigan Pioneer and Historical Society, Collections,* XXVI (1894-95), 274-297.

Fuller, George N. "An Introduction to the Settlement of Southern Michigan, 1815-1835." *Michigan Pioneer and Historical Society, Collections,* XXXVIII (1912), 539-579.

Hamil, Fred Coyne. "Early Shipping and Land Transportation on the Lower Thames." *Ontario Historical Society, Papers and Records,* XXXIV (1942), 3-19.

Osband, Melvin D. "My Recollections of Pioneers and Pioneer

Life in Nankin." *Michigan Pioneer and Historical Society, Collections*, XIV (1889), 431-483.

Scott, William A. " The Monetary System of the United States." *Encyclopedia Americana*. 30 vols.; New York and Chicago: Americana Corporation, 1941. XIX, 349-350.

Trowbridge, Charles C. " Detroit Past and Present in Relation to its Social and Physical Condition." *Michigan Pioneer and Historical Society, Collections*, I (1874-76), 371-385.

Turner, Frederick. " The Colonization of the West, 1820-1830." *American Historical Review*, XI (1906), 303-327.

Utley, H. M. " Plymouth." *Michigan Pioneer and Historical Society, Collections*, I (1874-76), 444-448.

Walker, Captain Augustus. " Early Days on the Lakes, with an Account of the Cholera Visitation of 1832." *Buffalo Historical Society, Publications*, V (1902), 287-318.

Webber, William L. " Indian Cession of 1819, Made By the Treaty of Saginaw." *Michigan Pioneer and Historical Society, Collections*, XXVI (1894-95), 517-534.

Williams, B. O. " Early Michigan, Sketch of the Life of Oliver Williams and Family." *Michigan Pioneer and Historical Society, Collections*, II (1879), 36-40.

Williams, Ephraim S. " The Treaty of Saginaw in the Year 1819." *Michigan Pioneer and Historical Society, Collections*, VII (1884), 262-270.

Youngman, Elmer H. " Banking in the United States." *Encyclopedia Americana*. 30 vols.; New York and Chicago: Americana Corporation, 1941. III, 168-175.

Index

164

Designed by G. Alden Smith
Text in Garamond, Chapter Heads in Bulmer
Printed on Warren Old Style Antique Wove
Bound in Holliston Roxite, Linen Finish
Printed and Bound by J. H. Furst Company, Baltimore, Maryland